Good Practice Guide: **Painless Financial Management**

RIBA Good Practice Guides

Other titles in this series:

Starting a Practice, by Simon Foxell (2006)

Negotiating the Planning Maze, by John Collins and Philip Moren (2006)

Keeping Out of Trouble, by Owen Luder, 3rd edition (2006)

Employment, by Brian Gegg and David Sharp (2006)

Fees, by Roland Phillips (2008)

Good Practice Guide:
Painless Financial Management

Brian Pinder-Ayres, Shepheard Epstein & Hunter

RIBA Publishing

Published by RIBA Publishing, 15 Bonhill Street, London EC2P 2EA

ISBN 978 1 85946 289 8

Stock Code 63509

British Library Cataloguing-in-Publication Data
A catalogue record for this book is available from the British Library.

Publisher: Steven Cross
Commissioning Editor: John Elkington
Project Editor: Alasdair Deas
Editor: Andrea Platts
Designed by Ben Millbank
Typeset by Academic + Technical, Bristol
Printed and bound by MPG Books Ltd, Bodmin, Cornwall

RIBA Publishing is part of RIBA Enterprises Ltd.
www.ribaenterprises.com

Series foreword

The *RIBA Good Practice Guide* series has been specifically developed to provide architects, and other construction professionals, with practical advice and guidance on a range of topics that affect them, and the management of their business, on a day-to-day basis.

All of the guides in the series are written in an easy-to-read, straightforward style. The guides are not meant to be definitive texts on the particular subject in question, but each guide will be the reader's first point of reference, offering them a quick overview of the key points and then providing them with a 'route map' for finding further, more detailed information. Where appropriate, checklists, tables, diagrams and case studies will be included to aid ease of use.

RIBA Good Practice Guide: Painless Financial Management

It may be a cliché but we as architects are neither educated to understand financial management nor apparently inclined to be bothered with it. All our learned impulses, energy and creativity are channelled into designing the best building we can; yes, to the satisfaction of the client but as often with a loftier ambition to improve the world.

However, we also have other professional responsibilities, many of which compel compromise and seem to thwart this design vision. Not least among these is the need to manage our finances so that we may continue to design at our best. In a business where plans need to be continuously updated to accommodate inherent unpredictability and yet where costs roll in relentlessly, any antipathy to dealing with balancing the books is doubly challenging. Architects have a choice – be subject to other people's cost-based decisions, or be sufficiently on top of the subject to manage the tension between design and cost and thereby safeguard quality through their own imagination and skill.

The joy of this book is that Brian Pinder-Ayres, a chartered management accountant, acknowledges this central tension and indeed faces it head on with invaluable, straightforward and easily adopted advice. His accounting experience from both architecture and other industries, combined with his friendly, sympathetic writing style, make this a first-rate blueprint for application in architectural practices both large and small.

Sunand Prasad
President, RIBA

Preface

Over the course of twenty-five years, I have had the great good fortune to work with a variety of different professional firms, helping them with the management of the financial side of their practices. I have worked with management consultants, property advisors, accountants and solicitors and, for the past ten years, with architects.

At some point early in the initial conversations, I have become used to hearing a phrase something like 'Of course, it's much more difficult for us in this profession, we face problems that you simply do not find anywhere else'.

I became accustomed to smiling politely while thinking to myself 'That's what they all say, but actually it always comes down to the selling of professional time and expertise – and then making sure that you get paid for it'. So it came as no great surprise when I heard a similar comment in my early days of working with architects, and I quietly dismissed the idea as usual.

After ten happy, exciting and challenging years working with my architect colleagues I have to confess that I have changed my mind and now I am ready to agree – it really is different in architecture! Architects face unique challenges, which stem from the intrinsic nature of construction projects, with their long timescales and complex programmes. Experience soon teaches us that most projects overrun their time and cost budgets, often very significantly, and that they will change and evolve constantly along the way, sometimes out of all recognition.

This all spells trouble for the potential financial health of the architect whose fee payments are based on the achievement of defined stages of the work as it was originally planned. Project change usually means project delay, and this has an inevitable knock-on effect in delaying the payment of fees.

The practice's outgoings, on the other hand, roll up with relentless regularity. The monthly payroll, the rent or mortgage, income tax and VAT and all of the other major costs that are involved in the running of the practice have to be met as they fall due.

So, this is the core of the problem – how can the practice's finances be kept on an even keel when the inflow of money is subject to so many possible delays, while the outflow of money is regular and unforgiving and largely beyond our control in the short term?

This guide attempts to show the ways in which this ever-changing challenge can be met.

Brian Pinder-Ayres

About the author

Brian Pinder-Ayres qualified as a chartered management accountant in 1984 while working with Mobil North Sea. He has held senior roles in finance with Polaroid, Braxton Associates (the strategy consulting arm of Deloittes) and a firm of specialist City solicitors. He worked for five years as a management consultant with chartered accountants Moores Rowland, during which time he specialised in advising professional firms on a wide variety of financial management issues.

He joined YRM architects just after their successful management buy-out in 1997 and established the finance function for the new business. In 2001 he took up his current role as Finance Director at architects and planners Shepheard Epstein & Hunter. He lectures regularly to Part 3 students on Finance in Architectural Practice at the Universities of Portsmouth and Cambridge and the South Bank in London.

Acknowledgements

One of the things that has often struck me in working with architects over the years is their openness and generosity. I have always appreciated their willingness to take the time to share their knowledge and experience of practice, often in the form of amusing or terrifying anecdotes.

I am deeply indebted to my fellow directors and colleagues at Shepheard Epstein & Hunter and to the directors of YRM architects for all of their help, advice and support. I am well aware that much of what I have learned, and which I am now putting forward in this guide, originally came from them. I have also learned a lot from the feedback of the Part 3 students and lecturers who have attended my lectures on this subject at the Universities of the South Bank in London, Portsmouth and Cambridge. Their questions and comments have helped me to focus on the areas of practice that are uppermost in their minds and to identify the most important areas to discuss.

I would also like to acknowledge all of the help that I have received from John Elkington and Matthew Thompson at RIBA Publishing. I have appreciated their constant encouragement and their patient willingness to answer a stream of naïve questions from an anxious first-timer.

Thanks, too, to Richard Brindley, Director of Professional Services at the RIBA for his enthusiasm and energy in bringing the whole *Good Practice Guide* series into being. Roland Phillips, who is the author of the companion guide on Fees, was kind enough to read an early draft and offer valuable advice and suggestions for improvement, particularly in regard to the new RIBA Standard Agreements.

Finally, I must say a big thank-you to my wife, Liz, who has been a constant source of encouragement and support throughout the whole project.

Brian Pinder-Ayres

Contents

Section 1
The challenge of architectural practice

In this Section:

- *A healthy tension*
- *Control of working capital*
- *So how can we accelerate the working capital cycle?*
- *Multi-level management*

The practice of architecture demands a far wider set of skills than is generally required in the pursuit of other professions. Successful lawyers will have developed sharp analytical skills that will allow them to follow principle and precedent in the logical pursuit of the argument in their case. The law touches every aspect of our lives, but the application of these skills is much the same no matter which area of the law an individual may chose to practise. The successful accountant will obviously have a facility with figures and an ability to 'think with numbers'. Hopefully, this will be coupled with an ability to communicate the significance of the figures to colleagues in other disciplines. Once again, the potential number of fields of application are many but the core skills remain much the same.

In contrast, the successful architect has to have the skills to be equally at home with 'blue sky' conceptual design or the production of detail drawings with tolerances of only a couple of millimetres. They will need to be able to come up with and visualise a building or scheme that could affect the lives of thousands of people over many years. Furthermore, they will need to be able to communicate that vision to potential clients. This communication has to be sufficiently dynamic and exciting to persuade the clients to invest large sums of money in the concept. They may well have to perform this miracle of inspiration with little more than a quick, outline sketch consisting of a bare dozen hand-drawn lines on a piece of blank paper.

Yet, at the same time, they will need to be able to perform repetitive tasks with great accuracy. They will have to be able to produce schedules of windows or doors that will be in tune with the overall design, and actually fit when they are delivered to the site. They will also need to have an understanding of the nature and qualities of the materials that are being specified and an appreciation of the environmental implications of the choices made in this area. These are all quite different skills, yet the successful architect will be required to have a command of them all. This is especially true for architects in small practices, where the limited number of staff precludes specialisation in particular areas.

This illustrates the underlying nature of the many challenges to be found in practice. Architects need to be able to accommodate a wide range of people and situations. They must be able to reconcile conflicting agendas and demands to achieve the balance that will lead to a practical solution. The architect stands alone on the podium with baton in hand and attempts to bring the orchestra of clients, planners, contractors, engineers, surveyors and staff together to produce a wonderful symphony. All this, despite the fact that all these groups have different music in front of them and never seem to be playing all at the same time!

Within architectural practice these conflicts must constantly be managed, and this is reflected in the financial management of the practice too. As with any other business, the fundamental aim is to define the desired financial destination and to steer a course towards it as steadily as possible.

However, as the following sections illustrate, many potential sources of difficulty lie in wait to drive the best-laid plans completely off course at any time. In the case of an aeroplane making a transatlantic flight, which is apparently technically off course about 80 per cent of the time, it is the pilot's job to keep making corrections so that everyone arrives, as intended, in New York rather than in Miami. So we, too, have to be constantly vigilant and prepared to make the necessary corrections to our financial journey along the way.

Our job is to develop a set of tools and indicators that will tell us quickly if we are going off course, and where we need to look to find a solution to the problem.

A healthy tension

In its purest form, the design process is a classic 'right-brain' activity. This term derives from the work of the American psychologist Roger Sperry in the late 1960s. He identified two types of thinking which he described as being either 'right brain' or 'left brain'. Right-brain thinking is visual and processes information in an intuitive and simultaneous way. It is a top-down approach, looking first at the whole picture before turning to the details. By contrast, left-brain thinking is verbal and processes information in an analytical and sequential way. It is a bottom-up approach that works by building up a sense of the whole from the detail of its parts. Many artists and architects naturally favour the right-brain approach to thinking.

When we are in right-brain mode we often enter a zone in which we lose touch with the outside world while fully engaged in a task, and a common characteristic of this condition is a sense of having lost track of time.

Actually, this is something we would generally wish to encourage. At the initial design stage we want our architectural designers to be at their creative best, unconstrained by too many practical considerations. The grounding process can come later, as the big ideas are translated into workable real world solutions.

As finance professionals, we live in a left-brain dominated world. The world of money is inextricably linked with the effects of the passage of time. Most of our costs are measured and accumulated on a time-driven basis. We need to pay our staff and our rent or mortgage monthly. We need to pay our utility bills quarterly and our professional indemnity insurance and professional subscriptions annually, and so on for every cost that we incur.

We prepare a five-year plan from which we derive our annual budget. From the budget we get our monthly forecasts of income and expenditure and consequent cash flow. This may lead, in turn, to weekly plans showing the projects on which staff are going to be spending their time. We are constantly aware of the relationship between time and money.

Thus, a tension arises. We expect and want our architect colleagues to 'lose track of time' and to get carried away with the excitement of the creative process. It is in this mode that they are the most likely to produce their best work.

Yet, we are also acutely aware that our financial obligations accrue relentlessly on a daily basis and that it is our responsibility to ensure that we will have the funds available to meet them when they become due.

So, a major part of the financial management role is the creation and management of a healthy tension. Without damaging or distracting from the creative process, we need to be constantly reminding the team that there are time and budget constraints within which we all have to operate. Ultimately, we will have failed if we end up with the most wonderful design that we cannot realise because we have bankrupted the practice in the process.

We need to create an atmosphere in which innovative design can flourish. But it must also be clearly understood that there is usually simply not enough time or budget to go through the process two or three times before settling on a design solution. We need to guard against a failure to complete the design process at the appropriate stage of the project. I have seen the consequences of designing 'on the hoof' at the working drawings stage. This is bound to result in change and confusion, which will lead to delay and additional cost.

Control of working capital

One of our key tasks in the financial management of the practice is the control of working capital. The total amount of money invested is known as the capital of the business. Some of this will be used to provide the permanent or fixed assets that are required, such as buildings, vehicles, furniture or computer equipment. The rest goes to provide the funds to pay staff and bills as they fall due. This is our everyday working money and is what we mean by working capital.

Working capital is often defined as the value of all current assets less the value of current liabilities. These are the terms used in the preparation of the annual balance sheet, so it is possible to calculate working capital by looking at the most recently prepared set of accounts.

Current assets include the cash balance at the bank, the value of money owed to us by our customers (our debtors) and the value of the work completed for which invoices have not yet been raised (which we used to call 'work in progress', but which should now, more correctly, be described as 'accrued income').

Current liabilities are the amounts that we owe to other people – mainly our suppliers but also the tax authorities for VAT, PAYE and National Insurance, and income or corporation tax. It will also include the bank if we have a short-term loan or overdraft. These people and institutions all allow us some time to settle our obligations with them and are extending some credit to us, thus they are known collectively as our creditors.

In summary:

Working capital $=$ cash $+$ debtors $+$ accrued income $-$ creditors

In other words, it is the money we have in the bank, plus the money that is owed to us by our customers, plus the value of the work completed but not yet invoiced, less the amount we owe to our suppliers.

The key to managing working capital successfully is to find the right balance between liquidity and profitability. If we were to employ extra staff we could undertake larger projects, which would hopefully result in greater profits. However, extra staff cost money and could prove to be very expensive if there are periods between projects when they cannot be usefully employed on fee-earning work. Again, we have a conflict of objectives and a tension to be managed.

How much working capital we need is determined by the overall level of our fees. We can divide our annual fee income by the value of working capital to work out how many times the working capital circulated or 'turned over' in the year. This is a good measure of how efficiently the practice is managing its financial resources.

Example:

Total practice fee income $=$ £200,000

Average working capital $=$ £40,000

In the above example the working capital circulated five times during the year, which could also be expressed as a relationship of 20 per cent. We can now predict that if we were to increase our fees by a further £50,000 we would require another 20 per cent of working capital, i.e. £10,000. This can be met in part from the extra cash generated by the additional sales, but will probably also require an increase in the short-term borrowing or overdraft facility. This, of course, comes at a cost and begins to have a negative effect on our profitability.

However, there is another way to tackle the level of working capital requirement. We can reduce the amount of working capital required by accelerating the rate at which money circulates in the business. In our example, the money in the business turned over five times in the year, which equates to a working capital cycle of 73 days. If we could speed up this process so that the money turned over ten times, we would reduce the cycle to 36 days but also reduce the requirement to £20,000. In other words, the faster that the money owed by clients is collected, the less working capital will be needed.

This is a crucial idea to understand. It means that two otherwise identical practices could require quite different levels of working capital, depending entirely on the efficiency with which they can manage the circulation of their working capital.

So how can we accelerate the working capital cycle?

By far the most effective way is to ensure that completed project work is billed promptly and regularly and that the resulting invoices are collected and converted into cash in the bank as rapidly as possible. We can assist the process to a degree by carefully taking advantage of all of the credit that our suppliers are prepared to give us. However, this is a limited process as there are costs involved in taking this too far. Taxes paid late will attract fines and interest charges, and suppliers have a statutory right to punitive interest charges if their agreed payment terms are exceeded, unless otherwise specifically agreed in their contract.

See also
Section 10
Credit control,
page 71

We will be exploring how we can do these things in Section 10 of this guide.

Multi-level management

We need to manage the practice on a number of different levels simultaneously. We need to be able to track financial performance at the project level, but also at the client or group level as well as the overall practice level.

We want to ensure that the majority of our projects are more than covering their costs and are making a financial contribution to the running costs of the practice as a whole. We need to add up these contributions from all of the current projects to ensure that, in total, they will be sufficient to cover the overhead costs and generate enough profit to be reinvested in the growth and development of the practice. We need to ensure that we have allowed the time and budget to undertake projects which will not make much profit or, indeed, may cost us money to carry out. It is wise to devote some time and resources to the competitive tendering process as competition is fierce and only high-quality submissions are likely to win. It is important to offer staff the opportunity to enter design competitions to enable them to exercise and develop their design skills at an early stage in their careers.

So, once again, we see the need to manage conflicting demands and to deal with the financial consequences of this conflict. Our aim is to create a financial environment in which the architectural practice can flourish. All of the architects that I have met have been far more concerned about the quality of the finished design than about making money. So, it is our overriding goal in financial management to ensure that money flows smoothly and steadily through the business, so that a lack of funds does not become a constraint on the growth and development of the practice.

SUMMARY

- Architects need a wider skills set than most other professionals as they need to be able to deal with the detail and the 'big picture' simultaneously.
- Architects have to be able to cope with a wide variety of people who have differing agendas and priorities. The need for diplomatic handling of conflict is key, and this is reflected in our approach to financial management.
- We need to maintain a healthy tension between the creative 'right-brain' nature of the design process and the 'left-brain' world of finance, where a time-is-money mentality rules.
- One of our primary tasks is the management of the working capital cycle. Whatever we can do to speed up the rate at which money flows through the business will reduce the total amount of money that we need to finance the business.
- We need to manage the finances of the practice at a project level and a whole firm level simultaneously to ensure that our overall financial objectives are met and to allow the practice to flourish and grow unhampered by financial constraints.

Section 2
Starting in practice

In this Section:

- *Sole trader and partnership*
- *Limited liability partnership (LLP)*
- *Limited company*
- *Raising finance*

Starting in practice is a major, and probably life-changing, decision and there are many factors to be considered. This section will focus on the financial aspects and, in particular, the significance and implications of the choice of business form. For a detailed examination of the whole process, readers are directed to the companion title in this series – *Starting a Practice*.

The initial choice of business form will have fundamental implications for the practice throughout its life, and will ultimately be of significance to the individual when it comes to leaving or retiring.

See also:
Section 11
Leaving
practice, page
81

Sole trader and partnership

The simplest business form in which to practise is as a sole trader or a group of sole traders who form a partnership. Each of the individuals involved is self-employed and responsible for their own tax affairs. Once you are registered as self-employed, you are ready to 'trade'. It is important to register with the tax office within three months of starting, otherwise a £100 penalty could apply. This is not a great way to start your self-employed relationship with Her Majesty's Revenue and Customs (HMRC). For an individual architect starting out on their own this is usually the sensible place to begin.

The great disadvantage of this business form is the potentially unlimited personal liability that it involves. Although you must have professional indemnity insurance (PII) in place in any event to be able to practise, there is always the possibility of a 'doomsday scenario' arising, where a successful claim against you exceeds your PII cover level. In these circumstances it is possible to lose all of your personal assets, including your home.

Many architects practised as partnerships for years and managed to sleep at night despite the 'joint and several' liability that is a key ingredient of the partnership mix. Sadly, the increasingly litigious world in which we now all live makes this an unacceptably risky model. It is widely known that professionals will have PII, and it is widely assumed that they also have deep pockets. This has made us all into potentially attractive targets. The solicitors and accountants who made up the profit-sharing ownership of the big firms became especially concerned about this issue, and they were the ones who led the campaign for the introduction of a new hybrid business model.

Limited liability partnership (LLP)

In many ways this new business form is an attempt to give the professional in practice the best of both worlds. Created by the Limited Liability Partnerships Act 2000, the partnership structure and ethos can be retained, yet the LLP also has the all-important protection of limited liability, conveyed by its separate legal entity status. In simple terms, it means that the partners will not all risk losing their homes and other assets in the event of a successful claim against the practice that exceeds the level of insurance cover.

As a consequence, the majority of the top 50 firms of solicitors and accountants have either already converted or are in the process of converting to LLP status. Traditionally, it was the fear of facing a large professional indemnity claim that kept people awake at night. But, in a recent survey of law firms which had converted, the reason most commonly cited for conversion to LLP was the fear of the potentially unlimited damages that can result from an employment-related unfair dismissal or discrimination claim.

Unsurprisingly then, this trend is also spreading rapidly to the other people-based professions and a significant number of architects are currently making the same conversion decision. I would expect to see many others follow suit in the next few years. Indeed, if I were advising someone contemplating establishing a new architectural practice today, I would strongly urge them to consider the potential benefits offered by the LLP.

The partners in an LLP continue to be treated for tax purposes as before, and carry on with the familiar regime of income tax paid via the self-assessment system. They do not need to trouble themselves with the adjustment in thinking that is required of the limited company director, who has to become used to the corporation tax regime, and to the delayed receipt of part of their remuneration package as dividends.

One of the consequences of becoming an LLP is the requirement to file financial information annually at Companies House. This step into the public domain will be a first for many and is sometimes cited as a reason to remain 'private', as a sole trader or partnership. Many partners have been concerned that their peers and staff will be able to see how much (or, perhaps even worse, how little) they have been earning. However, Companies House is well aware of the commercial sensitivities and allows for highly abbreviated accounts information to be filed for all but the biggest companies or LLPs. For most small businesses, and hence the majority of architects, this amounts to a basic balance sheet with a few requisite technical notes being made available to the public. In most cases it is very hard to deduce anything significant from these figures, in terms of how well the practice is doing or how much any individual is earning.

Limited company

The traditional alternative to working as a sole practitioner or partnership was to form a limited company. As the practice grows in size and the amounts of money involved become more substantial, a point tends to be reached where it makes sense to everyone involved to seek the protection of limited personal liability which is provided by setting up a separate legal entity. The level of financial risk starts to feel uncomfortable to everyone.

The operation of a limited company does involve a degree of extra formality and the need to ensure compliance with the requirements of Companies House and the HMRC. Recent legislation, in the form of the Companies Act 2006, has been designed to simplify and modernise some aspects of the running of a limited company. However, there will always be a price to be paid in terms of disclosure and public reporting in return for the benefit of limited liability. Companies House has the task of keeping records on every company on its register so that any creditor or other interested party can always find out where a company is based, who owns it and the identity of its directors. In order to ensure that this information is kept up to date, it has the power to fine companies for the late submission of information. In extreme cases, it has the power to take legal action against individual directors.

Some architects find it difficult to move from the informal culture of a partnership to the more structured world of the limited company. Hence, the appeal of the LLP, as described above.

In a limited company the ownership of the practice is reflected by the holding of shares. Shares can offer very useful flexibility, as circumstances change over the course of time. The more senior directors can sell or transfer their shares to the next generation on a gradual basis as a part of a succession planning exercise.

However, dealing with the changes in practice ownership via shares can be fraught with difficulty. Unless you have a shareholders agreement in place that deals with all of the eventualities, some very difficult issues can arise that revolve around the methods used to place a value on the shares held. The outgoing director/shareholder will, of course, wish to maximise the value to be received for the shares being sold. Equally, the acquiring shareholders will wish to buy the shares for the lowest possible price. Both parties will agree that a 'fair' price should be paid. But this is where problems can begin, as each has quite different ideas of what a 'fair' method of calculation would be.

In order to avoid these problems, it is wise to ensure that all new shareholders sign up to an agreement that specifies exactly how shares will change hands and how the values to be used will be calculated.

Raising finance

One of the recurring themes of this guide is that architectural practices tend to require more working capital than other businesses of a similar size because of the extended time periods that are involved with construction projects. As a consequence, architects will need more initial capital and must constantly manage their cash flow very carefully if they are to keep out of trouble.

Experience shows that anyone starting a new business tends to be over-optimistic. We all tend to underestimate how long it will take our customers to become as excited about what we have to offer as we are ourselves. We all tend to think that our sales will build up more quickly than they actually do, and we also do not take into account how long it will take to actually get paid for the work that we have done.

Talking to bank managers on this subject can be very revealing. They are in the business of lending money to new businesses and they are generally very keen to do so. However, they are well aware of this misplaced optimism on the part of their potential customers in relation to cash flow, especially in the early months and years. In order to make adjustments for this 'exuberance factor', they will look at the projected sales line and discount it by one-third or one-half to see what the consequent cash-flow effect will be. This then gives them a much better indication of how much money the business is likely to find itself needing to borrow. They can then apply their own lending criteria to this adjusted set of figures to see if this is business that they wish to take on.

Most start-up businesses will aim to finance their working capital requirements by means of an overdraft facility. This is often the most sensible option. It is important to match the type of finance with the expenditure. It obviously makes sense to purchase property by using long-term finance, such as a mortgage. However, it is also sensible to purchase assets with a medium-term life span such as computers or furniture using a three- or five-year term loan, rather than by further extending the overdraft. Any mismatch of finance could be regretted when trading conditions become difficult and cash is tight.

Studies of businesses that have gone into insolvency reveal that only a few failed because they could not make a profit or had a poor business model. The vast majority that do go under simply run out of cash.

SUMMARY

- This whole area is covered extensively in the companion guide in this series entitled *Starting a Practice*.
- The choice of business form will have significant implications for the business from the outset. It will also affect the way that the owners can exit from the practice when the time comes to leave or retire.
- Trading as a self-employed sole trader or partnership is simple and straightforward but does come with unlimited personal liability.
- The limited liability company is the traditional solution to this problem, but this entails added complications in the form of compliance with the requirements of Companies House.
- The introduction of the limited liability partnership (LLP) offers a hybrid solution. Architects can retain the look and feel of a partnership, while enjoying the protective cloak of limited personal liability.
- All new businesses have to raise finance and most tend to be over-optimistic about the level of sales they will achieve in their early years. It is important to build this factor into the business plan and cash-flow forecast that is used to approach the bank for overdraft facilities. There is a danger that insufficient money will be made available from the outset, which could lead to problems in the early days of the practice.
- Most new businesses of any kind that fail, tend to do so because they run out of cash, rather than as a result of failing to run a profitable business.

Section 3
Firm foundations

In this Section:

- *The accounting process*
- *Monthly profit reporting*
- *Key performance indicators (KPIs)*
- *Cash-flow key performance indicator*

The most important function of financial management is the prediction of what lies ahead. What profits are we likely to make? Will we have enough cash to be able to operate in six or twelve months' time? This needs to be combined with an ability to communicate those forecasts to the management of the practice so that they can respond accordingly. However, we cannot make meaningful projections if we do not have accurate historical information available as our starting point. The accounting process has to tell us where we are now, and we need to have confidence in what we are being told. Everyone's faith in the numbers is soon shaken if there are glaring errors in the figures that are presented to them. We are going to construct a complex model of our future, and make major decisions based on these foundations, so they need to be sound.

The accounting process

Underpinning the whole financial process is the book-keeping system. It does not matter if you are a sole practitioner or working in a practice with hundreds of staff, there has to be some reliable way of keeping the financial score. This is required by law in any event to satisfy our tax reporting obligations. The smallest of practices with only a few people involved may well be able to get by using simple spreadsheets to record lists of income and expenditure that can be translated into a final set of accounts at the end of the year by an external accountant. Most practices with more than a handful of staff will choose to use an accounting software package which performs the mysteries of double entry book-keeping for them in the background. These packages will also produce a preliminary profit and loss account (P&L) and balance sheet. More sophisticated packages will combine accounting, time recording and project planning and reporting to provide an integrated approach to all of the financial aspects of the practice.

A good book-keeping system will be:

- simple to operate and maintain – entering information needs to be easy and the transition from one financial period or year to the next must be straightforward
- detailed – containing enough information to enable items to be found again easily
- logical – items of a similar nature will be grouped together (for example, the office expenses for gas, electricity and water will be next to each other in the accounts list rather than being spread out and mixed up with other types of expense)
- up to date – credibility is soon lost if financial information is presented that is immediately shown to be wrong because it does not reflect the current situation
- documented – each transaction should have a supporting document (for example, an invoice or receipt to authenticate what has been recorded).

We need to record information in a timely way and there are a number of activities that have to happen on a routine basis. These procedures build up over the course of the financial year to enable the production of the final output of the process – the financial statements or annual accounts. The transactions and events that have to be recorded and a suggested timescale for each are detailed below.

Daily

- Money received – whether it is in the form of cheques or direct electronic payment.
- Payments made – whether in the form of cash, cheque or bank transfer.
- Invoices raised and sent to clients.
- Invoices received from suppliers or other consultants.

Weekly

- Staff timesheets collected and entered.
- Petty cash summarised and recorded.

Monthly

- Payroll processing.
- Staff expenses collected and reimbursed.
- Bank reconciliation – ensuring that all of the items on the bank statement have been recorded and that the bank's records agree with yours about how much money is left at the end of the month.

Quarterly

- VAT returns.
- The management information package which is needed to satisfy the requirements of the bank. This will include a cash-flow forecast and a report on the forward order book.

See also Section 6 Fee forecasting, page 45

Monthly profit reporting

The gradual collection of all of this financial information is necessary to be able to produce a set of year-end accounts that will satisfy the requirements of all of the various stakeholders in the business (i.e. owners, staff and the tax authorities). However, this same information can also be used to provide management information to inform decisions about the operation of the practice during the course of the year.

There is a distinction to be drawn between the approach to the management accounting process, which produces information during the year, and the end-of-year financial accounting process. The latter aims to give a complete, 'true and fair view' of the business and is the definitive statement of what happened financially during the year. This is produced mainly for tax and Companies House compliance purposes and can often take a number of months to be produced. By contrast, the practice needs management information to be produced as soon after the period to which it relates as possible. Situations can change so rapidly within the practice that information relating to one month that is not available until, say, 21 days after the end of that month

FIGURE 3.1: *Monthly 'flash' profit and loss results – profit in the month and in the year to date compared with the budget*

£000	Jan. actual	Jan. budget	Variance	Year to date 10 months	Budget 10 months	Variance
Gross fees	150			1,650		
Non-recoverable sub-consultant fees	–10			–100		
Net fees	140	165	–25	1,550	1,500	50
Resource costs	85	90	5	950	800	–150
Overheads	42	40	–2	385	400	15
Net profit before tax	13	35	–22	215	300	–85

could be of little or no value. Indeed, it could even prove to be a hindrance because it could lead to decisions based on circumstances that no longer apply.

So, management information needs to be made available quickly to the people running the practice. I take the view that management figures must be available within three working days of the end of the month. The major elements must be reported as accurately as possible, but some of the detail may be glossed over at this stage.

In most practices the Pareto principle, or as it is also known the 80/20 rule, will apply. Pareto was an Italian economist who observed that 80 per cent of the income in his country went to 20 per cent of the people. Subsequent management thinkers realised that this idea has wide application and 80 per cent of the effect often comes from 20 per cent of the causes. In architectural practice we can get a good picture of our financial position if we can reasonably estimate the 'big three' numbers, i.e. sales income, staff expenses and overheads.

Expenditure on staff and premises will usually account for the majority of the regular monthly expenses, and these can be estimated with a fair degree of accuracy as soon as the month is complete. There is a conscious trade-off between speed and detailed accuracy.

Even the final financial statements cannot be said to represent an objective and truly accurate picture of events. In preparing these accounts we always have to make some assumptions and exercise judgement about what values to include.

Financial data only becomes useful information when it has been understood. It is important to consider the needs and preferences of the audience and to have an appreciation of how they assimilate information. The primary need is to communicate the big picture in as striking a way as possible. In order to achieve this, it is important to evolve a reporting format that works well for the right-brain thinking architects.

The monthly 'flash' profit and loss results chart shown in Figure 3.1 presents the financial data in an immediately accessible format. The report is a condensed summary of the profit and loss account, showing the performance in the previous month, together with the performance in the financial year to date (YTD) and comparing each with the budget. The differences between the actual and the budget figures for each of these time periods are shown in the variances column. Variances are expressed following the usual convention that a positive figure represents 'good news', such as higher income than expected or lower expenses. Conversely, a negative figure indicates 'bad news', such as a shortfall in income or an overrun on expenses.

The monthly result gives a high-level overview, focusing on just a few key elements of the business, so that it is immediately obvious if any areas of the practice are missing their targets and experiencing problems.

Income

Income is shown after making allowance for fees that are being collected on behalf of other members of the design team. It is important to ensure that we are only looking at the practice's own net fee income. The architect will often be appointed as lead consultant on a project and will administer the billing and collection of the fees of the quantity surveyor (QS) or the engineers. We must ensure that we are not seduced into complacency by a healthy-looking turnover figure that is flattered by the inclusion of fees that do not really belong to the practice.

Resource costs

This category includes all of the expenses that relate to people. In addition to the direct payroll costs, there are the add-on employer's costs of National Insurance contributions, the cost of benefit plans such as life cover, medical insurance, permanent health plans, and the cost of training programmes and recruitment.

Overheads

The term 'overheads' sweeps up all the other categories of expense into one large pot. It is very easy to become bogged down in the detail when it comes to overhead costs. It is important to review overheads from time to time to ensure that money is not being wasted. It is a good idea for all items of expenditure to belong to somebody in the organisation who is responsible for keeping it within a predetermined budget. It is, however, unlikely that a significant financial problem in an architectural practice is simply the result of spending too much on overheads. It is far more likely to be a structural issue, such as the wrong number or the wrong mix of people for the work that is in hand, which is causing a financial strain. It is all too easy to avoid facing up to these difficult issues by becoming immersed in an investigation into a minor overspend on stationery or telephone charges.

From the report we can quickly assimilate whether we are making a profit or not, where we are in relation to the budget and whether this is a temporary problem or a long-term issue.

In the example shown we can quickly scan the figures and draw the following conclusions.

- The month of January was a disappointing month with profits £22,000 below the figure that was in the budget. A shortage of fees was the main problem. A shortfall of £25,000 means that the net income is 15 per cent below the budget. Small savings on resource costs were partly lost by an overspend on overheads, but this made little difference to the overall result.
- The ten months of the financial year to date (YTD) – sadly, the cumulative position after ten months does not tell a happy story either. Profits are £85,000 lower than was planned in the budget at this stage but the reasons are different. Here, we see that the net fees are only a little off target, but the major variance is a significant overspend on resource costs. Although there are small overhead savings, these could do little to rectify the overall position.

Key performance indicators (KPIs)

Another way to help with the rapid comprehension of the current financial position is to track profitability KPIs as follows:

- turnover by director/partner

FIGURE 3.2: *Key performance indicators – the key measures of financial performance compared with the budget and with industry benchmarks*

	This month actual	This month budget	Benchmark	Year to date actual	Year to date budget	Benchmark
Turnover by director – £000	35	40	30	36	40	30
Turnover per fee earner – £000	4.5	6	5	4.8	6	5
Profit as percentage of turnover	12	15	15	11	15	15
Profit per director – £000	4.8	5	5	4.6	5	5
Profit per fee earner – £000	1.8	2	1	1.6	2	1
Liquidity – overdraft cover	1.8	2	2	3.5	2	2

- turnover by fee earner
- profit by director/partner
- profit by fee earner.

The key performance indicators chart (Figure 3.2) summarises the comparison of each of these figures against the budgeted values and also industry benchmarks that are published from the results of inter-firm comparison reports.

Figures are shown for the current month and for the financial year to date.

The first five measures are concerned with income and profit; the last indicator is a measure of liquidity, often quoted in bank overdraft agreements.

As with all ratio analysis, it is at its most useful when viewed in terms of a trend rather than as an isolated value. Circumstances may conspire to make the position at the end of a particular month unrepresentative of the general pattern. Looking at a KPI's performance over a nine- or twelve-month period will eliminate these sorts of anomalies. Each practice will develop its own preferences as to the KPIs that best suits its circumstances and that it wants to monitor on a regular basis.

Cash-flow key performance indicator

For most practices there will be no need to produce a full set of accounts, i.e. profit and loss (P&L) and balance sheet, every month. The profit and loss account is designed to tell us how we performed over a period of time, usually the twelve-month period that comprises our financial year. The balance sheet is a picture of the business as it exists at a particular point in time, usually at the end of the twelve-month profit and loss period.

For example, if our financial year runs for twelve months from 1 April to the following 31 March, then our P&L is expressed as being for the twelve-month period ending 31 March, whereas our balance sheet just shows the closing position as at 31 March.

The balance sheet is often analysed in terms of the ratios between its different parts. This sort of analysis allows us to see the extent to which the business is running on borrowed money rather than the money invested or retained from the profits of previous years. It shows whether there is a current liquidity problem. Will the business have the cash available to pay the staff and its suppliers as bills become due?

This approach is reflected by the inclusion of a liquidity KPI in the monthly review, along with the profitability KPIs described above, in the form of overdraft cover.

Overdraft cover is calculated as the amount owed to us by our clients divided by the current overdraft balance.

Example: Overdraft cover

Let us assume that the total amount due from our clients at the end of the month = £25,000, and the amount outstanding on the overdraft stands at £10,000 at that time. The calculation would be:

£25,000 divided by £10,000 = cover of 2.5 times

This means that we are owed well over twice as much money by our clients as we owe to the bank on the overdraft.

This is a measure that is favoured by many banks, and is often written into overdraft agreements as a condition of the granting and continuation of their facility. The usual requirement is for a minimum of two times cover – so, in the example above the test has been successfully met and the bank manager will be reassured that the bank's money is in safe hands.

By way of contrast let us take a different scenario.

Let us assume once more that our overdraft balance stands at £10,000 but this time we only have £12,500 owed to us by our customers.

The calculation now is:

£12,500 divided by £10,000 = cover of 1.25 times

This clearly fails the bank's criterion of two times cover, and would be likely to prompt the bank to ask some urgent and difficult questions. The bank will be concerned, and feel that it is bearing too much of the risk in this business. If this situation has persisted over a number of months and the bank's management has become sufficiently alarmed, the bank could decide to ask for its money back immediately by calling in the overdraft. This may well be the end of the road, as the practice is very unlikely to have the money available elsewhere to meet this demand.

Regular and accurate book-keeping will provide the information from which we can work out whether the practice is making an overall profit. By its nature the process is detailed and repetitive and does not naturally appeal to most right-brain dominated architects.

But it really *does* matter that it is done well, and not seen as a piece of time-wasting bureaucracy, because it provides a firm and reliable springboard from which to leap into the uncharted waters that are the prediction of our financial future.

SUMMARY

- Our key role is to look ahead and predict what the financial future holds for the practice. In order to do this we need to have an accurate picture of where we are now, and this is what the accounting process is designed to provide.

- The first requirement is for a sound book-keeping system that is simple to use and keep up to date. If the routine tasks that are required on a daily, weekly and month basis are maintained, it is easy to produce useful management information.

- There is a difference in approach when producing figures for management purposes as opposed to those produced to satisfy the legal requirements of HMRC and Companies House. The emphasis in the production of management information is on the speed of reporting and a degree of estimation is acceptable so long as the overall impression is accurately conveyed. We need to produce information that can facilitate rapid action to remedy a situation before it develops into too great a problem.

- If we have accurate figures detailing our income and outgoings on our people and property, we will already have a fairly good picture of the profitability of the practice in that period of time.

- Key performance indicators help us to assess quickly which areas, if any, are a problem and need to be addressed. KPIs cover not just measures of turnover and profits but also of financing and liquidity. Each practice can evolve its own KPIs to suit its particular market and organisational situation.

Section 4
Project reporting

In the management of the practice our aim is to ensure that we always have the financial resources available to allow us to do the sort of architectural work that we would like to do. It is a hard fact of commercial life that a practice will not be able to realise its creative potential unless sufficient attention is also paid to its business side.

In order to do this we must ensure that, after everything else has been paid, we make sufficient profit that can be retained in the business to sustain the practice. The best way to ensure that we arrive at the correct overall result at practice level is to monitor the performance of each project as it progresses and to react to problems on each project as they arise. Adopting the discipline of planning the financial outcome of each new project as it comes into the office, and then comparing its performance to that plan, offers a far better chance of achieving the overall result desired at the practice level.

It is often difficult to gather the necessary financial information at the outset of a new project. The elation that comes from having won the work carries over to a natural enthusiasm to get started on the design process. It is all too easy at this stage not to worry about what may seem to be peripheral paperwork. This is one of those occasions on which it is necessary to establish the balance of tension described in Section 1 between the design process and financial reality.

See also Section 1 The challenge of architectural practice, page 3

If we fail to establish at the outset what we intend to be paid for this project, and what we intend to spend to earn this fee, then there is a significant chance that we will eventually find ourselves at the end of the project with only a vague sense of whether the project was ever financially worthwhile.

It is essential that we take the time to think through the project plan in terms of the resources that will be needed for each stage and for how long. This can then be translated into a cost plan by work stage, against which we can monitor actual performance. Certain information must be known from the beginning.

- How much is the overall fee?
- Are there other members of the design team that need to be paid from this fee?
- Is there an agreed fee schedule?
- Is there a detailed resource plan showing who is allocated to the project on a week-by-week and stage-by-stage basis?
- Are there significant other expenses involved (such as travel, hotel or printing costs) that will need to be absorbed as a part of the fee?

If this information is not already in place, we must risk unpopularity by continuing to ask for it until we receive it. Once we do have the information, we can develop a financial performance model that can be used to monitor the project as it progresses.

The calculation of cost

The largest cost on a project of any size will be the architectural resources used – in other words, the cost of the people working on the job. This may also include the cost of architectural services that are being bought in on a temporary or contract basis. Architects are paid on a time basis – an annual salary is essentially a contract to purchase a package of professional hours over the course of twelve months. So, the logical way to measure the cost of our people is by a time-based calculation, and for this we need a time-recording system.

The detailed recording of time is one of those left-brain activities that does not come readily to many architects. The advent of electronic time recording systems has made the whole process much easier in recent years. Yet, in any practice, it seems that there will inevitably be about 10 per cent of any group of people who will always be late in submitting their timesheets (and expenses) regardless of the procedures in place. This is not restricted to architects, by the way; every professional services firm encounters the same sort of issue.

The most workable solution to bringing the minority of tardy timekeepers into line would seem to be an automated reminder system, backed up with tenacity and a sense of humour. It is, however, essential for the integrity of the costing system that all time is eventually recorded.

We need to develop a cost rate for each person expressed in terms of pounds per hour. The cost calculation needs to encompass not just the salary and any regular overtime payments, if applicable, but also the add-on costs of benefits and employer's National Insurance contributions (NICs).

A typical calculation is illustrated below.

Example: Annual costs

Base salary	£36,000
Employer's NICs	£3,940
RIBA/ARB subscriptions	£300
Life insurance	£150
Health insurance	£300
Total	£40,690

Next, we need to calculate the number of hours available for work in a year.

Assuming five weeks of paid leave, there are 47 working weeks in a year.

Deduct three further weeks for bank holidays and an allowance for sickness.

So, we have 44 weeks with, say, 35 hours per week = 1,540 hours per year.

Thus, the calculation of the cost of a standard hour for this person is as follows:

£40,690 divided by 1,540 hours = £26.42 per hour

Once established, the cost rate calculation can be performed for each member of staff. Problems can arise if individual rates are published as there is a close correlation with the underlying salary and pay differentials can be accidentally exposed. To avoid this problem I would recommend that a standard average cost rate is used that applies to each group of people (for example, all Part 3

FIGURE 4.1: *Project resource plan spreadsheet, showing how the cost profile is calculated for a project (the number of professional hours needed per person per month multiplied by their cost rates)*

Hours

	Jan.	Feb.	Mar.	Apr.	May	June	July	Aug.	Sep.
Director	50	40	40	5	24	25	50	5	2
Associate	95	125	125	55	95	50	95	55	8
Architect	290	350	350	200	500	350	290	200	76
Asst Arch.	400	500	500	262	600	250	400	262	92
Total	835	1015	1015	522	1219	675	835	522	178

Direct costs

	Cost rate per hour: £	Jan.	Feb.	Mar.	Apr.	May	June	July	Aug.	Sep.
Director	£50	2,500	2,000	2,000	250	1,200	1,250	2,500	250	100
Associate	£40	3,800	5,000	5,000	2,200	3,800	2,000	3,800	2,200	320
Architect	£30	8,700	10,500	10,500	6,000	15,000	10,500	8,700	6,000	2,280
Asst Arch.	£25	10,000	12,500	12,500	6,550	15,000	6,250	10,000	6,550	2,300
Total		£25,000	£30,000	£30,000	£15,000	£35,000	£20,000	£25,000	£15,000	£5,000
Cumulative total		£25,000	£55,000	£85,000	£100,000	£135,000	£155,000	£180,000	£195,000	£200,000

students are costed at £15.00 per hour). These rates will, of course, need to be recalculated when salaries change during the year.

This calculation uses just the elements that comprise the remuneration package; consequently, the result is described as the direct cost. It is also possible to add in an allowance for a share of the office overheads, which are known as indirect costs. This allowance can be calculated in a variety of ways, but is often derived by dividing the total overhead costs by the total number of planned chargeable hours. Thus, if all of the fee-earning staff perform the planned number of chargeable hours, then all the costs of the practice will be covered.

Other than for the very smallest of practices I prefer not to include indirect costs, as the calculation of these charges can be difficult and, since the calculation is forever changing, the results can be misleading. I would recommend the simpler 'contribution' approach. Using this method we take the direct resource costs, as calculated in the example, away from the fee and we are left with a 'contribution' to the rest of the overheads of the office. We need to ensure that the total contributions received from all of the projects over the course of the financial year are sufficient to cover the overheads and to provide the desired level of profit. This subject will be addressed in more detail later.

> *See also Section 9 Bringing it all together, page 65*

The 'direct cost' rate is different from the 'charge out' rate. Charge out rates should include an allowance for indirect costs, non-fee-earning time (i.e. practice administration, marketing and training) and also a project margin.

We can now work up a detailed project resource plan, as illustrated in Figure 4.1. This shows us the number of hours of each grade of person that we will need on a month-by-month basis. These hours are then translated into cost by multiplying by the appropriate cost rate.

These values can then be plotted on a graph, as shown in Figure 4.2, together with the projected fees, also shown on a month-by-month basis. This project performance chart allows us to see how the planned contribution (planned fee minus planned direct cost) builds up over the course of the project.

Project performance

As the project progresses, we can plot the actual figures.

FIGURE 4.2: *Project performance chart 1 – a financial overview of the project at the outset*

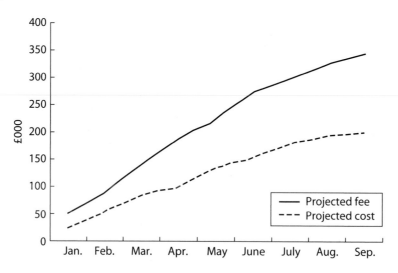

The project performance chart shown in Figure 4.3 illustrates the same project but with its actual fees added. From this we can see immediately where the project has deviated from the original plan. The purpose of this chart is to allow us to see problems as they arise in a clear graphic format. This should

FIGURE 4.3: *Project performance chart 2 – actual fees tracked against projected fees*

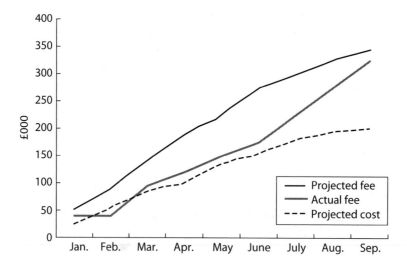

FIGURE 4.4: *Project performance chart 3 – actual fees and costs tracked against the projections*

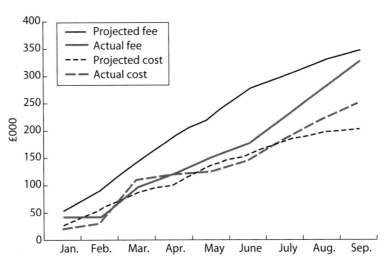

prompt an investigation of the situation until the cause of the deviation is understood. This graphic approach means that many projects can be reviewed quickly. Hopefully, most will be more or less on track and not require any further attention. Our time can then be spent managing those projects that seem to be going off course.

Figure 4.4 completes the picture for this example project by adding the actual costs extracted from the time recording system. This example does not make for happy reading. The final fee has turned out to be less than was originally planned, whereas the actual cost has turned out to be well over the original estimate. Consequently, the planned contribution of £145,000 has been reduced to an actual contribution of only £75,000.

These charts tell us when something is not going to plan, but this does not necessarily mean that things are going wrong. A squeezing of the planned contribution, as demonstrated by the narrowing of the gap between the actual fee and cost lines, is prima facie evidence of a problem. Yet it may simply be that the client has expanded the scope of the work and therefore more people have been working on the project than was intended. As long as we remember to negotiate an additional fee for this work, this is potentially good news for the practice.

Over the course of time these project profiles can grow into a useful reference library. We can build up information and start to look for patterns and trends. Do we experience particularly high or low levels of contribution in particular sectors or types of project? We soon learn that it is hard to make good levels of contribution on small-scale projects and that our profits tend to come from the larger projects in the office. We need to try to ensure that we maintain a healthy mixture of both.

Project performance is particularly prone to the effects of practice myth and rumour. I know of a practice that used to have its own conventional wisdom that hotel work was unprofitable and should be avoided. Hotel work was duly turned away for the next few years. Yet, when some brave soul undertook to analyse the actual figures on projects that had been completed, it emerged that the work on hotels had been of average profitability after all. It is often surprising to discover that projects which 'everybody knows' are unprofitable, may not actually turn out to be so when some real historic data becomes available for analysis.

Every project is different and one of the few things that we can say with any certainty is that situations and problems will arise that no one could have ever imagined at the outset. It is therefore important to have a monitoring tool available so that the financial effect of these events can be seen and responded to as rapidly as possible.

I have always encouraged the sharing of project performance information with the team working on the job. People enjoy the sense of involvement that this brings, and it allows them to understand how their own activity fits into and affects the project performance overall. People take their work to heart and like to be a part of a successful project. If we provide them with an awareness of the job's ongoing status, there is far more chance that they will align their own performance with the overall needs of the project.

SUMMARY

- Overall practice profitability is only likely to be achieved if individual projects are targeted and monitored. By ensuring that the majority of our projects stay on track and deliver the profit that we planned for them to make at the outset, we have a far greater chance of ending up with a profitable business.
- The first step is to find a way to understand what it is costing us to carry out the work. We need to develop a method of calculation that will tell us the cost per hour for each person who is working on the job.
- We need to develop a detailed resource plan that shows the people we need and the periods of time for which we need them. Then we can apply the hourly cost rates to come up with an overall cost for the project.
- We can monitor the actual performance of the project against the plan as the project progresses. This can be achieved most easily using a chart or some other form of graphic reporting. This allows us to quickly pass over those projects that are on course and to concentrate our attention on the few that are not.
- Sharing information with the members of the team gives them a sense of involvement and responsibility and will allow them to align their own actions with the best interests of the project overall.

Section 5
Long- and short-term planning

In this Section:

- *The five-year plan*
- *The annual budget*
- *Zero-base budgeting*
- *Identifying the key or limiting factor*
- *Flexible budgets*
- *Capital expenditure budgets*
- *Budgets for the sole practitioner or small practice*

Having got the accounting foundations in place, so that we know where we are and how we got here, we can then have the confidence to turn our attention to the future. Armed with the knowledge of our past performance, we can start to predict what we expect or would like to happen next.

It is important to have a long-term plan. Occasionally, we need to break free in our thinking from the tyranny of the accounting year. Although the twelve-month financial period is a natural and convenient period of time to use, it can result in an unhealthy focus on the short-term view. This is a problem for many businesses, but is particularly out of step with the long-term nature of construction projects.

The five-year plan

In my experience, there is a strong correlation between those businesses that are financially successful and those where the management team have taken the

FIGURE 5.1: *Five-year plan performance targets*

	Current year	Year 1	Year 2	Year 3	Year 4	Year 5
Sales: £m	1.2	1.5	1.8	2.0	2.2	2.4
Profit before tax: £000	72	105	144	180	220	240
Profit: %	6	7	8	9	10	10
Number of qualified staff	10	12	14	16	18	20
Healthcare as percentage of sales	5	7	9	10	12	12

time to develop and share a vision of where the business will be in five or ten years' time. The RIBA Small Practice Survey 2007 indicated that practices who have business plans are more profitable (achieving upper quartile performance) than practices who do not have this financial planning in place. The practice that has worked out what it has to offer that is special or different, and has identified the sort of client who would be attracted by that sort of service, has gone a long way to ensuring that it is likely to succeed. Thus, the annual budget process should ideally be preceded by the development of a long-term, five- or ten-year plan.

This plan needs to outline the strategic objectives for the business, and then express them, year by year, as a series of measurable targets or benchmarks that can be monitored.

Let us assume that our practice has identified the following strategic objectives:

• to double the size of the practice
• to improve profitability by 10 per cent
• to expand within the healthcare sector.

Figure 5.1 shows the key performance targets that have been selected to be monitored across the five years of the plan. If these measures remain on track, then it is safe to assume that the practice will be achieving its strategic objectives.

This is a small enough range of targets to be monitored regularly. There should be an annual review and feedback report which gives a clear indication of the progress being made.

Most professionals, including may architects, often seem reluctant to engage with a long-term planning process and find it difficult to escape from the 'noise' of day-to-day practice. It can seem like a great indulgence to take time out for 'blue sky' thinking and debate. There is often an anxiety that arises when we ask ourselves to look beyond the immediate future. We all fear the potential embarrassment of setting out a grand plan and then publicly failing to achieve it. Yet those who undertake this sort of exercise regularly, are convinced of its benefits.

We seem to lose sight of the fact that even when the exercise is complete, bound and published this is still only a plan. This is not to say that we should abandon the plan at the first sign of trouble, but, equally, we are not inextricably bound to it and the plan could (and should) be revisited and revised in the light of experience.

It is obviously a worthwhile exercise to define the direction in which we would like the practice to go. The younger architects in the practice will look to their directors or partners to provide clear guidance on the ethos and design aspirations of the firm for which they are working. I have always been impressed by the desire of young architects to have a wider appreciation of the work that they are doing and by their hunger to understand how their work fits into the practice's design philosophy and mission. They want to work and they want to learn but they also want to feel that they are part of a larger architectural vision and purpose.

In the absence of a plan, there is a strong possibility that we will be taken in whatever direction events happen to lead us.

The annual budget

Having settled on the five-year plan and broken it down into annual targets, we are now ready to tackle the budget for the coming year. It is logical to use the actual results of the previous financial year as a starting point, but it is also important to ensure that we do not simply carry forward and incorporate past errors.

Many expenditure budgets are prepared by just adding an inflation factor to the previous year's value. This is an easy, but not always helpful or intelligent, way to approach the exercise. It may be a reasonable approach with some routine items, such as utility costs, but it is dangerous to simply apply it across the board.

Zero-base budgeting

It is a good idea to go through a 'zero-base' budget exercise every few years. The idea of the 'zero base' is to ignore the current situation and all its commitments and to start with a blank sheet of paper. We ask ourselves the question:

If we were just starting out in practice again today how would we go about it?

This approach involves taking a critical look at every item of expenditure and asking difficult and searching questions, such as:

- Do we really need to spend this money?
- What would be the implications if we did not spend this money at all?
- Could we get more or less the same result if we were just to spend, say, 50 or 75 per cent of the current amount?
- Is there another, less expensive, way to achieve the same result?

This can be a challenging but rewarding exercise. Many practices do not invest the time in the budget process that it deserves, and consequently they miss out on its very significant benefits.

For example, we could consider the amount spent on the office rent or mortgage. Normally, this would not be given any attention in the budget process as it is simply taken as a fixed cost. Given that, frequently, there are break clauses only every five years in rental agreements, this is often true in the short to medium term, but we should still try asking the zero-base questions and see where they lead us.

- Do we really need an office of this size?
- Does it really need to be in this location?
- Is there more scope for people to work flexibly, perhaps from home?
- Do we make best use of the available technology to make flexible working as easy as possible?
- Would hot-desking work for us?
- Could we outsource some work?
- Why are we renting when we could be buying? (or vice versa).

This can be a liberating intellectual process that forces us to consider how our practice really operates and how we would like to see it develop.

Identifying the key or limiting factor

Having taken the turnover and profit targets for the coming year from the five-year plan, we now need to focus on identifying the one area that is most likely to make it difficult for our plans to be achieved. This is often referred to as the key or limiting factor. It is easy to assume that this factor will be the level of sales, i.e. will we be able to win and deliver enough work to be able to invoice our clients for the amount that we are targeting? But other factors can also be involved. Increasingly, in architecture, we find ourselves limited by the availability of people with the degree of skill and experience that is required. Some practices may be limited primarily by a lack of space or computer equipment or software.

It is important to identify this factor as it provides a starting point for the process. Let us assume that we have decided that the main issue is a shortage of people with the right skills. This leads us to consider how we can address this problem. We need to budget for expenditure on recruitment advertising or agency fees, but, probably more importantly, we also need to budget for the time that our current staff will spend interviewing and administering the recruitment activity. In architectural practice we need to budget our people's time carefully, as this is our key resource and the main thing that we have to sell. We need to allow time for marketing activities and professional training and development. A number of the senior people will have a variety of responsibilities for managing the practice and this, too, has to be taken into account. However, we also need to ensure that, across the practice overall, we have enough time available to deliver the required level of project work.

Budgets work best when those in the practice have a sense of ownership of the final result. Budgets that are imposed without any consultation by a remote management team are likely to be resented and resisted. The process should begin with the various individuals or groups being invited to make a budget proposal of what they would like to spend and why. It is useful to invite them to a budget review meeting where their ideas can be discussed and where they can present the 'business case' for the money that they would like the practice to spend. It must, however, be clear that these can only be proposals until the budget is finalised. It is frequently the case that, when you add together all the proposals for expenditure from the various budget holders, they total 150 per cent or more of the available funds.

Our job is to reconcile the top-down approach that comes from the targets for the financial year set by the five-year plan, with the bottom-up approach that comes from the individual budget holders or groups. The identification of the limiting factor will help us to decide where our efforts, resources and money can best be used.

Once the process has been completed, it is important that each person or group involved receives feedback on their submission. They will need to understand why their submission has been approved or amended in the context of the overall budget for the year. Hopefully, they will be able to appreciate how their individual budget will fit into the goals of the practice as a whole.

Flexible budgets

Once the budget for the year is agreed and published, it becomes an authority to spend the money that has been approved. As expenditure arises it should be approved by the appropriate budget holder before it is processed for payment. The budget holder should also receive regular feedback, perhaps once a quarter, on what they have spent and how the expenditure in their area compares to the budget.

However, there is a danger that, if the level of overall activity is far greater or less than was anticipated, the approved levels of budgeted expenditure will no longer 'fit'. We need to review the actual financial results on a quarterly basis and decide if we need to 'flex' or adjust the budget accordingly. It will obviously be a problem to maintain expenditure at the agreed level if fee income is 25 per cent lower than anticipated. Equally, however, it would be problematic to maintain the original budget level of expenditure when fee income is 25 per cent higher than expected. This is likely to require some support in the form of extra expenditure.

These later adjustments should be a fine-tuning exercise rather than a repeat of the whole process. We should not simply abandon the original budget, but rather update it as the year progresses with refinements in selected areas.

Figure 5.2 is an example of an annual operating budget. It shows the amount of profit which the practice plans to make in the year and compares this year both with the previous year's actual performance and with the original budget for the previous year.

Capital expenditure budgets

For accounting purposes, a distinction is drawn between revenue and capital expenditure. Capital expenditure is the money spent on items that are long term in nature and will remain in use in the business for longer than the

FIGURE 5.2: *Annual budget for the twelve months ending 31 March*

	Budget: £000	Previous year actual: £000	Previous year budget: £000
Gross architecture fees	2,500	2,355	2,400
Other income	15	12	–
Total income	2,515	2,367	2,400
Less			
Sub-consultant costs	125	115	50
Net income	2,390	2,252	2,350
Project-related resource costs	1,250	1,305	1,275
Non-project-related resource costs	355	400	300
Total resource costs	1,605	1,705	1,575
Other expenditure			
Property costs	225	215	210
Office costs	275	300	275
Insurance incl. PII	40	45	45
Travel and entertainment	50	55	35
Advertising and promotion	45	40	45
Legal and professional	25	20	25
Other expenses	15	15	15
Total other expenditure	675	690	650
Operating profit before tax	110	–143	125
Interest costs or income	15	20	16
Profit before tax	95	–163	109
Corporation tax at, say, 20%	22	–29	25
Profit after tax	88	–114	100

current financial year. Examples of capital items are vehicles, furniture and computer equipment.

In architectural practice there is a continuous need to upgrade and replace computers to ensure that they can operate the increasingly sophisticated drawing and modelling software as it becomes available. Failure to use the most up-to-date software could pose a serious threat to the practice's ability to compete for work. Clients have ever-rising levels of expectation when it comes to the quality of presentation and visualisation material they want to see from their architects. What was considered to be cutting-edge graphics technology two years ago is now expected as standard. If a practice failed to employ the latest techniques that others were using in their presentations, clients would notice and draw their own conclusions. As electronic drawings and 3D models become more complex, they require increasing amounts of electronic storage space. This means that money also needs to be spent continually on servers and back-up facilities. We need to budget for the expenditure that will be required to allow the practice to function effectively in this area.

One of the key reasons that an adequate level of profit is vital is to provide the funding for this sort of reinvestment in the business. By their nature, capital expenditure budgets are often prepared on a medium- to long-term basis. From this plan, the capital expenditure budget for the coming year can be agreed and integrated into the annual budget process.

Figure 5.3 is an example capital expenditure budget, showing the amount of money that the practice has agreed to devote to long-term expenditure. The items detailed are not included in the annual profit and loss account as they will have a value for the business for several years.

The value of each item is charged gradually to the profit and loss account over a number of years in the form of depreciation.

FIGURE 5.3: *Capital expenditure budget for the year ending 31 March*

Proposed spend in the year: £		
IT equipment		
Projector for client presentations	2,000	
3 new printers	3,600	
Graphics card upgrades	3,000	
7 new computers – rolling update programme	11,900	
Expand capacity of e-mail server	5,500	
		£26,000
Office improvements		
Reception area upgrade	2,000	
Replace entrance screen	2,000	
Kitchen refurbishment	3,000	
Office lighting improvement	2,500	
		£9,500
Overall total		£35,500

Budgets for the sole practitioner or small practice

Those working in a smaller practice, or perhaps on their own, may be wondering how they can apply these ideas. As with all of the various tools and methods described in this guide, the underlying principles remain the same, regardless of the size of the practice. I feel that even the smallest of practices could benefit from having some version of all of the tools and reports described. Judgement is needed, of course, in deciding how to scale and adapt each of the particular techniques to suit the smaller practice.

I would certainly recommend that every practice, even sole practitioners, should set aside some time to work out and write down a three- or five-year strategic plan, and to then produce a budget for the coming year accordingly. I believe that it is very important to end up with a written plan and budget, as this forces us to be clearer and more decisive in our thinking. The plan become more 'real' when it is given a physical form.

It is always a fascinating exercise to go back to an earlier statement of intent to compare what has actually happened with what we had planned. It is also surprising, and often quite revealing, to revisit the original plan or budget and remind ourselves of what it actually said. Our memory can make subtle adjustments to our recollections over time, and it is interesting to take note of where this has occurred as it gives us clues as to our areas of weakness and our financial blind spots.

The budget provides a map of the financial journey ahead and a point of reference for comparison purposes along the way. The pay-off for investing in this process comes when the comparisons to the plan or budget prompt us to ask questions that we would not have asked otherwise. This is more likely to lead us to the real source of the problem rather than relying on our feelings or instincts, which are coloured by our preconceptions or prejudices.

SUMMARY

- Given firm accounting foundations, we can start to look to the future, which is the main purpose of the budget process. It is designed to provide a way for us to determine our own destiny, rather than being at the mercy of whatever our current clients would like us to do.
- Successful businesses of any kind usually have a strategic, long-term plan and the management team shares a vision of what and where the business will be in five or ten years' time. This is then translated into a five-year business plan.
- The annual budget is derived from the five-year plan and describes what is going to happen in the coming twelve months, as an aid to achieving the long-term goals.
- It can be useful to adopt a zero-base approach to the budget process every few years. This is a challenging exercise, which starts by taking nothing for granted and asking if each of the things on which we spend our money is really necessary.
- Every practice will need to identify its key or limiting factor. This is the single most important element determining whether we are going to be successful in achieving our budget targets. Often, the limiting factor will be our ability to achieve the desired level of sales, but it could also involve having the correct mix of people, or sufficient space or technological resources.
- Budgets need to be kept under review on a quarterly or half-yearly basis. It may be necessary to 'flex' or adjust the budget if a far higher or lower level of activity has resulted than was originally planned. This does not mean that the original budget is abandoned, but rather that it is scaled up or down as appropriate.
- Large-scale capital expenditure also needs to be budgeted, and this must be integrated into the process.

Section 6
Fee forecasting

In this Section:

- *Future captive fees*
- *Future possible fees*
- *Combined fee forecast*

At this point we should know where we are, how we got here and where we want to go next. I have always promoted the idea that accounting is more of an art than a science – indeed, the picture of the past that it paints is much more in the style of the Impressionists than the Realists.

Financial statements have a comforting and seductive air of accuracy and authority. Yet, those of us who have been involved in their production know that there has been considerable scope for judgement and interpretation in putting the numbers together. This means that the resulting figures are the best approximation of the business situation as we see it. Others may have taken quite a different view and would have produced an equally 'accurate', yet dissimilar, set of results.

The accountancy bodies have worked for many years to produce a series of standards that will result in financial statements being produced in a consistent fashion. This quest has been expanded to a global level with the recent emergence of a set of international accounting standards. Yet the problem remains that businesses are so diverse that it is impossible to formulate a single set of rules that will apply in all cases. Hence, there will always be a need for judgement and differences of opinion and approach.

Future captive fees

So, if arriving at an accurate image of the past is so difficult, how are we to approach the task of working out what the future will hold. The starting point

FIGURE 6.1: *Captive fees forecast – contractually agreed fees for current projects*

Project	Apr.	May	June	July	Aug.	Sep.	Total	Future years
				£000				
Project A	75	75	50	10			210	150
Project B	50	50	75	100	25	25	325	250
Project C	25	25		15			65	
Project D	10	10	10	10	10	10	60	
Project E	75	20	15	20			130	
Total	235	180	150	155	35	35	790	400

has to be the prospects for future income represented, in the architect's case, by a schedule of future fees.

Figure 6.1 shows the fees which the practice plans to invoice in the coming twelve months. This is the best indicator of how busy the practice is going to be in the short to medium term.

You will note that this report shows fees that are described as 'captive'. This means that they are agreed, fully documented, contractually binding and scheduled fees for current projects. Only when they have achieved this degree of certainty are they allowed onto this chart. Prior to achieving that status, they form part of the mixed bag of 'possible fees' described below.

Figure 6.1 shows, on an individual project basis, the fees that we expect to be able to invoice on a monthly basis. These are then added to arrive at a total for each month. In our example, six months are shown, but in practice this would probably be extended to twelve months or more.

As the year elapses we replace the forecast figures with the actual figures achieved and revise the balance of the forecast accordingly. It is a revealing exercise to compare the forecast billing in each month with the actual figures to see what differences arose.

As we have noted earlier, our ability to invoice is often delayed by events on the project that are beyond our control. Consequently, we often find that we need to slide a fee profile sideways across the chart, indicating that we will be raising those invoices in later months. It is useful to take steps to stop this process from becoming too 'slippery'. If a culture arises in the practice whereby it is considered acceptable, or even expected, for fee schedules to slip, this can lead to a dangerous short-term cash-flow position. It is good practice to promote a culture of fee commitment in which everyone understands that an entry on the captive fees schedule is taken as a promise to deliver that fee for the benefit of the practice in that particular month. Fee slippage is then viewed in a poor light and discouraged by peer pressure.

As with most financial reports, it is most easily read from the bottom up. From the budget process we will have calculated what our monthly expenses are and have a monthly cash break-even figure in mind. (The cash break-even figure is simply the accounting break-even figure with non-cash items such as depreciation added back.) We can quickly scan across the months and see if there is a problem. Let us assume in our example that the cash break-even figure is £180,000. We see that April and May are fine, but there is currently a problem in June and July and we would like to see more fees in that column to at least bring us up to the £180,000 figure. Beyond that, August and September are currently a long way short. If the forecast proved to be the way things actually turned out we would have a serious problem!

Happily, the gloomy scenario predicted for six months or so ahead never seems to catch up with us. This chart typically has a 'cliff edge' profile, as illustrated in Figure 6.2.

FIGURE 6.2: *Captive fees – the 'cliff edge'*

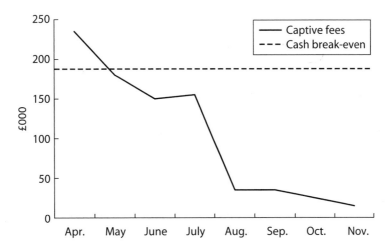

This profile reflects our normal work winning/delivery cycle. Most architects find themselves in the position of being too busy right now, reasonably busy for the next few months and then seriously short of work thereafter. The trick is to ensure that the 'cliff edge' does not advance any closer. As long as we can keep our captive fees forecast at break-even level or above for about the next six months, all will be well. If the 'cliff edge' does start to become uncomfortably close, say only two or three months away, that is the time to devote substantial energy to the sales and marketing front, to see if any of the possible jobs that have been incubating for some time can be encouraged to hatch.

The comfortable position for the cliff edge will vary for each practice, depending on the nature of its work. Practices working on smaller and more sudden 'quick-fire' projects can be comfortable with a cliff edge of, say, three to six months. For a practice focusing on larger, longer term projects that take longer to secure, such as hospitals or infrastructure projects, a cliff edge nearer than twelve months may indicate a real problem.

Future possible fees

As described above, all of those future fees that we hope to earn, which are anything other than completely certain, should only be classified as 'possibles'. This can often constitute quite a long list and may include many different projects and situations. These can range from a project that is all but won, but which is awaiting the final sign-off from the client, to a project in which we have done no more than express an initial interest. It is useful to keep a written record of all of these and to track their progress. Hopefully, there will be a gradual conversion process underway, taking projects from the possible list to the captive fees list.

The mixed nature of these projects presents us with a problem, as some are much more likely to become real jobs than others. We need to develop a way of quantifying the probability of winning each job, and thus arriving at some sort of weighted average total that can be compared from month to month.

Figure 6.3 estimates the likelihood of future fees levels by taking all of the potential work that is currently being pursued and applying a success probability factor to each project. All of these probability- and time-adjusted values are then totalled to produce a value that can be compared to the equivalent value in earlier months. The aim is to predict medium- to long-term fees.

FIGURE 6.3: *Possible fees forecast – estimated likely future fee levels*

Project	Project value: £000	Fee %	Fee: £000	Prob. %	Probable fee: £000	No. of years	Probable fee per year: £000
Project A	25,000	4	1,000	25	250	2	125
Project B	350	7	25	75	18	1	18
Project C	12,000	3	360	50	180	3	60
Project D	1,500	3	45	75	34	1	34
Project E	52,000	4	2,080	10	208	4	52
Project F	45,000	5	2,250	5	113	4	28
							$\underline{\underline{317}}$

The example shown in Figure 6.3 presents a wide variety of projects in terms of size, fee and likelihood of winning. Project A has a 25 per cent probability of success – this could be because we are on the final shortlist of four firms. Project B is shown with a 75 per cent probability of success. Perhaps this represents a new instruction from an existing client, where there is no other architect involved and hence no competition, but the project still needs budget approval before it can begin. Project F is considered to have just a 5 per cent chance of happening – perhaps this is a project that is just at the 'expression of interest' stage.

Furthermore, if these fees were to be won they would be earned over different periods of time. Some will happen in the coming year but others will only be earned over a number of years.

We need a method that attempts to reconcile these variables and give us an indicative value that can be compared from month to month, so that we can see if a trend is emerging. There is no 'right' way to do this and the method described below is just one possible suggested solution. Each practice should derive its own model to suit its particular needs based on its own experience. What is important is that some attempt is made to predict the future levels of fees that will result from all of the current marketing activity.

In this method we derive an adjusted value for each project by taking the fee value, applying the probability factor and then annualising it by dividing by the number of years.

Example: Possible fees forecast

Potential fee	£100,000
Estimated probability of winning	25%
Period over which fee will be earned	2 years
Annualised adjusted value =	£100,000 × 25% × 0.5 = £12,500

The same calculation is performed for each potential project, and a total figure is derived. In itself, this figure has no great meaning. However, when it is tracked over a number of months it can be a useful predictor of future fee levels. The resulting chart is shown in Figure 6.4.

The possible fees chart can be strangely cruel. Imagine that you have just won a major new project which you have been pursuing for some time. The successful team who were involved in the bid are applauded, the champagne is duly sipped, the design team is assembled and work begins.

FIGURE 6.4: *Possible fees chart – possible future fee levels over the coming months*

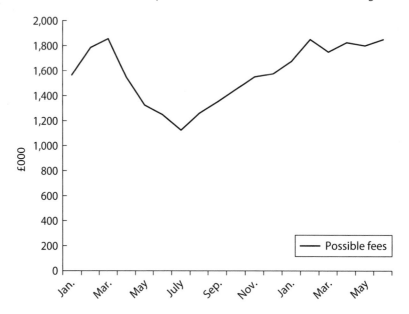

We then revisit our possible fees chart to update it a few days later and discover, to our dismay, that it is now plunging downwards. The winning of the job means that it has become a captive fee and has therefore disappeared from the possibles list and total. This serves to remind us of the harsh reality of our situation. It is great to have won some new work, but we must now set in motion the strategies that will win the work we need to keep us going in nine to twelve months' time.

Combined fee forecast

Smaller practices may find it helpful to prepare a combined fees forecast, as shown in Figure 6.5, which shows the overall fees picture on a month-by-month basis. It is of course important to continue to appreciate the distinction between those fees shown in the top half of the chart, which are already contractually agreed, and those in the bottom half, which we can only hope will happen.

As this example shows, the overall monthly totals seem to be reasonably consistent throughout the period of the forecast. However, in the latter months of August and September the forecast is still heavily dependent on fees that are yet to be confirmed and therefore we need to try to convert these into captive fees as soon as we can.

FIGURE 6.5: *Combined fees forecast*

Captive fees					£000			
Project	Apr.	May	June	July	Aug.	Sep.	Total	Future years
Project A	75	75	50	10			210	150
Project B	50	50	75	100	25	25	325	250
Project C	25	25		15			65	
Project D	10	10	10	10	10	10	60	
Project E	75	20	15	20			130	
Total captive fees	235	180	150	155	35	35	790	400
Possible fees								
Project X	15	15	10				40	
Project Y	20	25	25	15	45	45	175	125
Project X				25	75	90	190	75
Total possible fees	35	40	35	40	120	135	405	200
Combined total fees	270	220	185	195	155	170	1195	600

Combining these two fee forecasts can give a good idea of how busy we are going to be in the short to medium term. We can see whether we need to put more resources to do the work that we have on hand, or perhaps step up the marketing drive in place to ensure a flow of new work in the future.

SUMMARY

- In order to have an idea of how busy we will be in the future, we keep track of the potential fees that we have in hand that we can consider as firm or captive. This means that they are covered by a contractual agreement and are, as far as anyone can predict, definitely going to happen at a particular time.
- When shown on a graph, the captive fees tend to follow a familiar pattern. We know with reasonable certainty what we will be doing for the next three or six months, but beyond that we fall off the edge of the cliff to a level of fees that would not be sufficient to sustain the practice. Our constant mission is to ensure that this cliff edge does not come too close, but is kept at a constant distance in the future.
- All other potential fees are classified as possible fees. We need a way of converting all of the different levels of potential for winning these jobs into a single indicator that can be compared from month to month. This then gives us some sense of how much time we should be devoting to the marketing effort now in order to ensure that there is new work in the pipeline in nine or twelve months' time.
- The possible fees chart can be cruel. A job won transfers onto the captive fees chart and boosts those figures. However, this then leaves an equivalent hole in the possible fees chart, which will now show a downwards trend that will require new potential jobs to reverse.
- By monitoring these two measures we can obtain a good sense of the short- and medium-term prospects for work that can be invoiced. These charts need to be constantly updated as events change, if they are to retain their relevance. These charts tend to be on my desk all of the time, so that I can scribble in pencil amendments as they become known. I then update the spreadsheet properly once each week.
- Projects are often delayed or rescheduled and this will have a knock-on effect on fee billing, which needs to be kept under constant review.

Section 7
Resource forecasting

In this Section:

- *People allocation forecast*
- *Project resource forecast*
- *Project resource allocation*

The captive fees forecast described in Section 6 tells us how much work we have on hand and gives us a good idea of how full our forward order book is for the next three to six months. This information can then be linked directly to the cash inflow section of our cash-flow forecast, which gives us a prediction of our solvency position over the next nine to twelve months.

See also Section 6 Fee forecasting, page 45

What we now need to know is whether we will have the right number and mix of people available to be able to deliver the work we have lined up. We start this process by producing a people allocation forecast, as shown in Figure 7.1.

See also Section 8 Cash-flow forecasting, page 59

Figure 7.1 shows how work has been allocated to each individual person in the practice over the coming weeks. Our example is, of course, simplified for illustration purposes. In reality, people may well be working on a number of projects simultaneously.

The report takes account of people being away on holiday, study leave, sickness, etc. and these values are deducted in arriving at the 'people available' total. This total can then be carried forward to the project resource forecast, illustrated in Figure 7.2, which compares the total practice requirement with the total current availability in order to predict shortages or spare capacity.

This is a rolling weekly forecast of the number of people that will be needed on a project-by-project basis. This is then compared to the total number of

FIGURE 7.1: *People allocation forecast – people available for project work*

Name	Week ending	May 3	10	17	24	31	June 7	14
John		Project A			Holiday	Project A		
James		Project B		Project C		Marketing		
Sandra		Study	Project C					
Emily		Project A				Project C		
Jane		Project A			Project C		Holiday	Leaver
Total available for project work		4	5	5	4	4	3	3
Study		1	0	0	0	0	0	0
Holiday		0	0	0	1	0	1	0
Marketing		0	0	0	0	1	1	1
Total people		5	5	5	5	5	5	4

FIGURE 7.2: *Project resource forecast – the number of people required on current projects and predicted shortages or spare capacity*

Number of people required Week ending	May 3	10	17	24	31	June 7	14
Project A	4	4	4	4	3	3	2
Project B	2.5	3	3	1	1.5	0	0
Project C	3.5	3.5	3.5	4	2	2	1
Project D	2	2	2	1	3	3	3
Total required	12	12.5	12.5	10	9.5	8	6
Total available	14	14	12	12	12	10	10
Net position (surplus/shortage)	+2	+1.5	−0.5	+2	+2.5	+2	+4

FIGURE 7.3: *Project resource forecast plotted – the 'cliff face'*

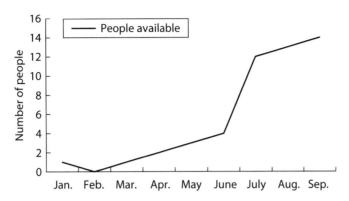

people available. From this report we can see immediately where we can expect shortages or surpluses to occur. It is prepared on a weekly basis to reflect the way that the resourcing needs of projects tend to fluctuate as the work progresses. Like the captive fees forecast, it needs to be updated continuously to reflect the inevitable changes that occur. These are not only project changes but people availability changes too.

This does require an individual within the practice to commit to investing their time in keeping the chart up to date. We find that this effort is well rewarded by providing an early warning system, allowing us to see resource problems coming a month or two ahead. This generally allows sufficient time to react and solve the problem before it becomes a crisis.

The project resource forecast will tend to echo the shape of the captive fees chart. But, whereas the captive fees chart could have its 'cliff edge' some six to nine months away, the resource chart will show a reverse pattern, with a 'cliff face', illustrated in Figure 7.3, that also appears in approximately six to nine months' time, when it appears that there will be a lot of people free with no project work to do.

It is important to plan for some flexibility, so that there are always people available to help with the general marketing effort, whether it be submissions for new work, working on design competitions or updating the practice's website or promotional material.

This can be very hard to achieve, especially when there is great pressure on teams to deliver against a deadline, but it is just another aspect of the constant need to keep winning work for the future to ensure that the practice can survive. The forecast may show that two people are allocated to 'marketing'. However, what this usually means is that, say, five people will each be spending some part of their time on these activities over the course of the week, blended in with their other activities. When all of these pieces of individual activity are aggregated, they will amount to the equivalent of two people working full time on the marketing front.

Like most of the charts in this guide, project resource forecasts are most useful for showing trends over time. They tend to follow a familiar pattern. There always seems to be more work to do now than people to do it. The weekly total column may well show −2 or −3, which means that we could really do with a couple of extra people right now and next week. However, it does seem that things will calm down after that and that balance will be restored – the chart total shows 0. So we have to get our heads down (again) for the next week or so to meet our deadlines. We are comforted by the knowledge that things will become easier soon, as the cavalry arrives in the form of people becoming free of their current project commitments – the chart perhaps starts to show +2 or +3. Then we hit the 'cliff face' in about six months' time, where it appears that most of the practice will be sitting around drinking coffee and reading magazines, waiting for the phone to ring.

In reality, this tends to be a fairly constant situation. As new, smaller pieces of work filter in, or current projects expand or change, there is always more to do now than we had anticipated. So when we see a consistent number of weeks with a −2 or −4 total ahead, we then know that it is time to look for some extra people. This may either be through the recruitment of permanent employees or by arranging temporary resources to meet specific project deadlines.

Experience teaches us that projects rarely run to their expected timetable. They can suddenly accelerate when a client makes a project change or brings a deadline forward or be temporarily frozen, as the result of an unexpected delay occurring in gaining a planning consent, or funding not becoming available at the time that it is expected. Each of these events causes a rapid shift in the resources balance and the need for some swift revisions to the plan.

As well as the capacity to deal with project and client changes, an additional factor to consider is the need to accommodate the aspirations of the individual architect or design team. Understandably, the individual is looking for the stimulation of new challenges and to gain experience in a variety of building types across a range of sectors. Yet, from the practice's point of view, the most efficient way to resource a project is to use people who have recent experience of working on a similar sort of project. They will have gained expertise that will enable them to deliver a good result quickly and efficiently, which, of course, also means at a lower cost.

The need to manage this potential conflict successfully makes the resource planning process critical to the success of the practice. It requires a detailed knowledge of how projects work, complemented by a sensitivity to the needs and desires of the individuals involved, combined with an intuitive feel for how a particular group of people will function as a team. Getting the balance right is quite a feat to keep pulling off every week.

Frustratingly, once this elusive balance is achieved, the chances are that something will come along to upset it within a matter of days, so that the whole plan will need to be reviewed in order to reach a new balance.

We learn from the competitive tendering process that clients tend to want architects with a strong, recent track record. When commissioning a new hospital, it is entirely understandable that the client will choose an architect who has successfully built three hospitals in the past two years over another, equally competent, architect who has built only one hospital in the past ten years.

So, as a practice, we tend to win the same sort of work that we have won before. Equally understandably, our own staff want to work on a variety of different building types in a number of different sectors. They may become bored and dispirited if they feel they are becoming typecast in a particular sector or as a particular type of architect. Eventually, they may decide that they need to move on to another practice in order to further their development and career.

We may also need to develop a reporting procedure that documents our reasoning in making our resource allocation decisions to support our equal opportunities policies.

Resource forecasting is probably the hardest part of the whole process as it has to try to predict what the practice's people situation is going to be. People never cease to surprise us, especially the sort of intelligent, young creative people that we find in the architecture world.

Yet it is still very important to try to predict and control this area, as such a large proportion of the practice's finances are invested in it – just be prepared for a bumpy ride!

SUMMARY

- As well as having a sense of what work we will have in the future, we also need a way to predict whether we will have enough people with the right level of skills available to deliver that work. This is the function of resource planning.
- Resources also need to be planned for all of the other essential but non-fee-earning tasks, especially marketing. It is a constant challenge to maintain the right balance between delivering the work that we have in hand and ensuring that there will be sufficient work to do in six or nine months' time.
- Resource planning needs to take account of the professional aspirations of the individual architect. From the practice's point of view, it may be most efficient to allocate people to the sort of work that they have done before. However, the individual is likely to be looking for variety and new experience in order to further their knowledge and expertise. Once again, this is a potential conflict that needs to be carefully managed.
- Resource prediction is the most difficult part of the whole process of financial forecasting, but it is vital as so much of our money is invested in this area.

Section 8
Cash-flow forecasting

In this Section:

- *Cash inflows*
- *Cash outflows*

Accountants and bank managers love cash-flow forecasts. The reason that they like them so much is because they know that they are the most accurate way to predict the future of the business, in both the short and medium terms. Accountants know from their experience of dealing with insolvency that most businesses fail simply because they run out of cash. The popular misconception is that businesses become insolvent because they fail to make a profit or find sufficient customers. The truth is that the majority are forced to close because they could no longer meet their financial obligations as they fell due and the bank's goodwill had been exhausted.

You will commonly hear the directors of a recently declared insolvent company say things like 'If only that major customer had paid us on time, then we would have survived'. Indeed, insolvency can also be the direct result of success. The receipt of a major new order or the winning of a significantly large piece of new business can result in 'overtrading'. This is a situation where the business does not have the working capital to cope with the increased volume of activity and consequently cannot meets its obligations.

Another factor contributing to the failure of many practices is 'the dreaded quarterly VAT payment', so called because it is often the final straw. It is the last large payment that simply cannot be met, which pushes a business that has been teetering on the edge of its overdraft limit for the past few months over the edge.

FIGURE 8.1: *Cash-flow forecast – the amounts of money predicted to flow in and out of the practice each month and the projected closing bank balance*

	May	June	July	August	Sept.	October	Totals
				£000			
Opening balance	−32	88	45	55	39	−60	
Fees collected (60 days)	250	145	175	155	165	225	
VAT collected	12	15	18	16	18	20	
Total cash inflows	262	160	193	171	183	245	1,214
Net payroll	66	68	70	75	75	75	
PAYE/NI	26	27	28	30	30	30	
Rent and service charge	12	12	15	12	12	15	
Prof. indemnity insurance	0	7	7	7	7	7	
Sub-consultant payments	5	5	5	5	5	5	
Supplier payments	30	30	30	30	30	30	
Input VAT	3	3	3	3	3	3	
VAT payment	0	50	0	0	45	0	
Corporation tax	0	0	0	0	50	0	
Capital expenditure	0	0	25	25	25	25	
Total cash outflows	142	202	183	187	282	190	1,187
Closing balance	88	45	55	39	−60	−5	
	May	June	July	August	Sept.	October	

So the cash-flow forecast is the most important tool that we have for predicting the continuing financial health of the practice. A typical cash-flow forecast, detailing the amount of money predicted to flow in and out of the practice in the course of a month is shown in Figure 8.1. This is the classic report prepared by finance people all over the world and the bank manager's favourite.

Like many financial reports, these can most easily be read from the bottom up. The line at the foot of the page shows us the predicted closing bank balance at the end of each month. This tells us immediately if we have an impending problem, and when it is likely to arrive.

It is worth looking at the forecast in some detail to see how we arrive at the figures.

Cash inflows

This is the money coming into the practice, of which the largest element is the collection of fees from clients. We need to establish a realistic assumption about how quickly our fees are collected. Our standard payment terms may be 30 days, but that does not mean that is what we usually achieve. We need to judge the reality of the situation based on experience, which can be done by the calculation of 'debtor days' as follows:

Annual fee income   £200,000

Average amount due from clients (debtors)   £33,000

£33,000 divided by £200,000 × 365 = 60 days (approximately)

i.e. on average it takes 60 days to collect the fees that we invoice.

This then becomes our working assumption to be used for cash-flow purposes. So, we can fill in the 'fees collected' row by taking the figures from our captive fees forecast and entering them into the cash-flow two months later. This means that fees invoiced in January will be assumed to be collected in March, and so on.

For the cash-flow forecast we need to account for all of the money going in and out of the practice, so we have to allow for the effects of VAT. Assuming that our clients are UK based, we need to add 17.5 per cent to the fees collected as an inflow. We need to estimate how much VAT we pay to our suppliers and enter that figure as an outflow. Then we need to plan for the payment of the net VAT difference (i.e. VAT collected on sales less VAT paid on purchases) on a quarterly basis. As already mentioned, it is very important to be prepared for this large payment that falls due to HMRC every three months.

Cash outflows

The first thing to notice on Figure 8.1 is that there are many more rows in the outflow section than there are in the inflow section. As in the rest of life, there always seems to be many more ways to spend money than there are to earn it. Even in this simple example there are a number of lines that represent groups of expenses. It is worth taking some time to ensure that all of the many forms of practice expenditure are included somewhere. It can be useful to pour over old bank statements or cheque stubs to look for items that have been missed or only arise occasionally, for example annual subscriptions or insurance renewals.

The largest cash outflow is likely to be the payroll. The income tax and National Insurance contributions that are deducted from salaries have to be paid over to HMRC by the 19th day of the following month. Thus, the total payroll figure for any given month is split between two months, with the net pay going out in the first month and the tax deductions in the next month. In the normal course of events this makes little difference, as the total outflow is much the same from month to month. However, it is important to model the effects of the annual pay review and the payment of any bonuses.

It is useful to identify significant single items, such as the professional indemnity premium, which may have to be paid in a single instalment or perhaps spread over a number of months, as shown in Figure 8.1. It is also helpful to identify the payments that need to be made to other members of the design team where the architect is acting as lead consultant for invoicing and payment purposes. These can be significant amounts and could have a serious impact on the cash-flow, especially if the architect ends up having to pay the consultant before having collected the equivalent funds from the client. This can represent a significant area of risk for which the architect usually receives little, if any, reward.

We need to ensure that we include those items of capital expenditure that were identified in the budget. Once again, these can require large sums to be spent at a particular point in time. The cash-flow forecast may lead us to consider entering into finance arrangements, such as leasing for the purchase of computer equipment if outright purchase would seem to be straining the cash-flow unduly.

See also
Section 5
Long- and
short-term
planning,
page 35

The payment of tax is yet another important item to include in the list of expenditure. For a partnership or LLP there will be self-assessment income tax payments to be made in January and July. For a company there will be an annual corporation tax payment to be made within nine months of the end of its financial year end.

In common with the captive and possible fees and resource charts, this is a rolling forecast. In this example, it is a rolling six-month forecast. This means that we revise the forecast each month and, in so doing, remove the first month (which has now become the current month) and add a new month on to the end. Each practice will need to establish a suitable forecast period to suit its own needs. For smaller practices it is likely to be up to six months, whereas larger practices may well be able to work meaningfully with a twelve- or eighteen-month forecast.

The example cash-flow shown is a normal operating model. If the practice is considering approaching the bank for the financing of a major project, such as the purchase of new premises or the acquisition of another practice, it will need to produce cash-flow forecasts that extend over two or three years in support of the application. For end-of-year accounting purposes, the accountants or auditors may request a similar long-term cash-flow forecast to support the 'going-concern' assumption for the business.

It is interesting to check the total value of inflows against outflows over the forecast period to get a sense of overall liquidity. In the example, total inflows over the six months are £1.214 million whereas the total outflows are expected to be £1.187 million, indicating a potentially balanced position. However, as this forecast is directly linked to the fee forecast described in Section 6, it will tend to follow a similar pattern. Most cash-flow forecasts show an improving position over the next quarter or two and then a rapid deterioration six months or so later. This reflects the uncertainty of future fees that practices all tend to face in the medium term.

> *See also Section 6 Fee forecasting, page 45*

The cash-flow forecast is one of the documents that the bank will want to see on a regular basis in support of its overdraft facilities and it is important to ensure that it is as accurate as possible. Banks do look back and review the accuracy of the cash-flow forecasts that they have been given. They understand that these are forecasts and will not be entirely correct. However, if they can see that the forecasts they have been given are consistently inaccurate, they will begin to have doubts about the competence of the management team and the practice's ability to manage its financial affairs. If the bank feels uncomfortable, it may be unwilling to renew the overdraft facility when it falls due, which could have serious implications as this situation could arise at very short notice.

Cash-flow is often described as the lifeblood of a business. It is useful to think of cash in these terms, as something that needs to keep circulating in order to keep all the parts of the practice healthy.

SUMMARY

- The cash-flow forecast is one of the most important financial control documents. If money has been loaned from the bank, it will certainly expect to see this forecast at regular intervals.
- A lack of solvency is the most frequent cause of business failure. It often comes as a surprise to learn that an apparently profitable and successful business or practice has gone into liquidation or receivership. This will simply be because they ran out of cash, rather than because they were unable to attract profitable business.
- Periodic payments like income tax or VAT, which occur on a quarterly or annual basis, are often the last straw. The practice may be just managing to keep its head above water, in financial terms, from month to month when a large tax bill becomes due, which simply cannot be paid.
- Cash-flow forecasts need to take account of other items such as capital expenditure on cars, computer equipment or furniture. These can require large amounts of cash to be found at a particular point in the year and could throw the whole forecast out if not planned for accordingly.
- Cash is the lifeblood of any business. It represents the flow of energy through the body of the practice. It needs to be kept moving and it needs to be constantly refreshed.

Section 9
Bringing it all together

In this Section:

- *Financial management in practice*
- *Turnover analysis*
- *Benchmarking*

The previous sections have covered the various individual tools that we can use to get an idea of how much work we will have, whether we will have the people to do that work and what it should all cost. From this information we can produce a cash-flow forecast that tells us whether our financial future will be a comfortable glide or a white-knuckle ride.

The process of successful financial management is somewhat like driving a car. You need to have the majority of your attention focused on the road ahead and what the other traffic (your clients and competitors) is doing. But you also need to be constantly glancing down at the dashboard to check that there are no warning lights flashing. When a light does show, you need to understand how serious the problem is – can you keep going for another few months and fix it later, or is it an urgent problem that could bring the whole practice to a sudden halt if not dealt with very soon.

The journey that we are planning to take is mapped out by the annual budget. Progress is monitored on a monthly basis by comparing where we are with where we planned to be at this time. This is the satellite navigation system with which we can get back on track from wherever we find ourselves.

The view through the windscreen of the road ahead is the captive fees forecast. This gives us the best indication of where we are going, how busy we are going to be and for how long. As we saw in Section 6, this chart tends to have a familiar shape to it. We can see clearly what we will be doing for the forthcoming month, and probably for a month or two after that. The next three months after that are sketched in, but the timing is much more subject to change. Beyond that period we may have fees totalling about 50 per cent of what we actually require planned, and then, after that, very little at all that is firmly committed. If this eventuality actually came about we would be out of business very rapidly. Most practices will have a forward order book profile that looks like this.

See also Section 6 Fee forecasting, page 45

In most cases, the cliff-edge tends to be six to nine months away. The trick is to ensure that it always remains that far away. If it creeps closer and becomes only three or four months away then we know that we need to get busy trying to convert some of those possible fees into captive fees. Larger practices may well have a 'cliff edge' that is 18 to 24 months away, whereas a small practice may only have three or four months of confirmed work in front of them at any given time.

Our list of 'possible fees', as described in Section 6, is our best indication of how much fuel we have in the tank. It aggregates all of the work that we have some chance of winning. This can range from projects that are all but won and just need a final sign-off or approval to become captive, to jobs where we are long-listed and are just one of perhaps nine or ten practices that are still being considered. This list of potential jobs is often quite long, which can be deceptively comforting. So we need to keep an eye on the trend of the line on the chart that attempts to factor in the probability of success for each job. If all we really have is a very long list of jobs that we are unlikely to win, then we are going to run into trouble in about six months' time.

See also Future possible fees, page 48

There is a long time lag between the first hint of a new job and the final winning of it, and we need to ensure that we are keeping the pipeline of prospective projects topped up on a constant basis.

Turnover analysis

As well as ensuring that we are growing the practice and making a profit, we also need to maintain the balance of the expenditure profile or relative shape of the practice. The turnover analysis chart in Figure 9.1 illustrates a way to do this.

FIGURE 9.1: *Turnover analysis – how the practice is spending its income compared with an industry benchmark target*

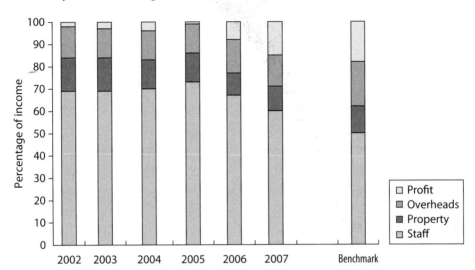

This chart analyses the turnover of the practice each year in terms of the percentage of the overall total that is spent in the main practice areas. These are the same 'big three' categories of cost that we used when preparing the monthly flash profit report in Section 3 – these are staff, premises and all other overheads.

The right-hand side of Figure 9.1 shows the target or benchmark performance that we are aiming for. In this example, we have defined the target profile as:

- staff – 50 per cent
- property – 12 per cent
- overheads – 20 per cent.

This leaves 18 per cent as profit or funds available to contribute to the future growth and development of the practice, shown as the top slice of the bar.

We then plot the actual performance year by year against it in the same format, which allows us to see very quickly if we are moving towards the benchmark, and, if we are not, to identify the area that seems to be 'out of shape'.

In our example we see that in the first year, 2002, this (fictitious) practice made only a very small percentage of profit – a mere 2 per cent. The problem is immediately apparent – far more was being spent on staff costs as a percentage than the target. Actually, the cost performance in the property and overheads categories was better than the target, but it was not enough to rescue the overall position.

Some small level of progress in the right direction is made in 2003 and 2004 but, again, this is achieved by the further squeezing of property and overhead cost rather than by addressing the proportion of total spend that is going on staff.

This situation reaches a crisis point in 2005. Although property and other overheads are again kept well down, the staff costs percentage increases once more and, as a result, almost no profit is made at all. This level of thin profitability is dangerous. At this level there are not enough spare funds being

See also
Capital
expenditure
budgets,
page 40

generated to provide the money that will be needed to replace and upgrade computer equipment. This will become an operational necessity very rapidly as the continual development of architectural software requires quicker and larger capacity machines to be able to function.

This seems to have finally prompted the management of the practice to take some remedial action. We see that in 2006 staff costs are finally reduced and a degree of profitability is restored. Further significant progress is made in 2007 and the practice turns in a very creditable 15 per cent profit performance.

It is important to appreciate that these are percentages and not absolute financial values. It is quite possible that the practice described above was enjoying rapid expansion in the years of very low profit margins. Almost all businesses find it hard to maintain their profit performance in terms of profit margin during a period of growth.

It is easy to see how this could happen in an expanding architectural practice. It is only natural when a practice wins a large new project that one of their first actions will be the recruitment of some new staff to help deliver the work. It is unlikely that the practice would have people ready and available just in case such a project were to arrive. Most practices tend to run a bit light on resources as there always seems to be just a bit more work on hand than was expected. So there can be something of a panic reaction, especially if this is a new client and the practice is keen to impress.

This is absolutely fine while the new project is in its early design stages and is at a labour-intensive phase. Yet, this time will pass and people will gradually be released from the project onto other work. They will probably have useful fee-earning work to do, but it may not be as profitable as the initial work on the major project. In this way, additional resource cost gets built into the practice, and the relative cost shape begins to suffer.

Another new project is won and the cycle repeats itself. Once again, six months later, we have built in even more staff cost. This may seem to be acceptable as we are increasing turnover, so it is only natural that our staff budget will be increasing too. It is only when we come to review the overall shape in percentage terms, as in Figure 9.1, that we discover the problem. It is a common experience for growing businesses to find that, despite a doubling of turnover, the amount of profit they have made has stayed the same or even fallen. This can be a source of great disappointment, prompting responses such as 'Why did we bother to do all of this extra work if we were only going to end up with the same amount in the end?'

The answer, of course, is to find a way to maintain the turnover at its new increased level, but to address the cost profile issues so that a satisfactory margin of profit is made. At the increased level, action to adjust the cost profile should produce a very healthy amount of money as a profit, which will provide the practice with opportunities and choices.

Benchmarking

While reviewing the performance of the practice at the overall level, it is interesting and instructive to see how other practices of a comparable size are performing. Participating in inter-firm comparison exercises is a great way to do this, and the RIBA has launched its own online service in this area in collaboration with the training and advisory company, Colander, which have been providing this service for a number of years.

This is an exciting development as it will allow each practice to get a different view of itself in relation to its peers. The survey covers all areas of practice and, although financial performance is covered extensively, there are also sections on marketing, the winning of work, use of technology and HR issues.

On a monthly basis we need to gather all of the various sources of information that we have assembled and put it together. Over time, we can become very skilled at drawing conclusions from all of the data we have in front of us. This will allow us to tackle problems at an early stage, when they should be easier to deal with.

SUMMARY

- Having developed a number of indicators to show us how the practice is doing and where we are going, we need to learn how to read all of these signals simultaneously, so as to avoid getting bogged down in any one problem area.
- We need to develop skills akin to driving a car, in which most of our attention is focused on the road ahead (our confirmed future fee income) while continuously glancing down at the fuel gauge (our potential fee income), the oil pressure (the cash-flow forecast) and the engine warning light (the resource forecast) and also looking in the mirror by comparing our current performance to the budget and our performance in previous years.
- It is important to keep an eye on the overall cost shape of the practice. Especially in periods of rapid growth, it is easy to allow a particular category of cost to become too great a proportion of the whole. In architecture we often see this with our people costs. Our natural tendency is to recruit when we win new projects, but we can accidentally build up staff numbers, and consequent cost, on a permanent basis if we do not keep this under review. It is useful to consider other forms of more short-term resourcing, sometimes utilising temporary or contract staff, or perhaps some form of outsourcing.
- It is helpful to refer to and to participate in inter-firm comparison or benchmarking exercises, such as the service now being offered by the RIBA. This covers all areas of practice and peer comparison, which can be very revealing.

Section 10
Credit control

In this Section:

- *Late payment*
- *Aged debtor report*
- *The 'drop-through' and 'multiplier' effects*
- *Resolving fee problems*

Having gone to all the trouble of winning a project, seeing the work through to the client's satisfaction and sending in the fee invoice, it is hard to understand why any architect would then neglect to ask for the bill to be paid. Yet it is surprising how often this seems to be the case. The professional time and effort to which the bill relates probably took place a number of months before, so why should we accept any further delay at the payment stage.

Good organisation is the key to effective credit control. The collection process does not need to be either aggressive or apologetic; it just needs to be done in a calm, regular and determined way until the desired result is achieved. There is still some reluctance among architects and many other professionals to talk to their clients about outstanding fees. There can be a sense that this sort of conversation will damage the relationship with the client. In fact, I have found the opposite to be true. Clients do not respect architects who do not run their own business affairs in a professional way. Indeed, they may wonder how professionally and efficiently their architect is dealing with their project and money, if they do not seem concerned about running their own practice in a business-like manner.

The credit control process should really begin before any design work has been done at all. Unless the client is known to you from a previous project or is a referral from a trusted source, it is wise to undertake some form of credit checking to see if they have a good record of keeping their payment promises. Companies such as Dun & Bradstreet and ICC provide reports that give an objective view of a potential client's creditworthiness, based on the experience of others. It is not just a question of whether they pay or not, it is also a matter of how quickly they pay. It could make quite a difference to your cash-flow if a major client routinely takes an average of 60 days to pay rather than 30.

As soon as you start to work for a client and allow professional time to be devoted to that client's project, you are effectively extending credit. You would not loan money from the practice's bank account to someone without first checking them out to see if they are able and likely to repay you. The same principle should apply in this situation, which is in fact exactly the same.

Once it has been established that the client is creditworthy, the credit control process begins with the negotiation of the contract. Most payment problems stem from a misunderstanding between the architect and the client. These misunderstandings may arise from uncertainty in one or all of these areas:

- the exact scope of the work to be done
- the precise terms of the contract
- the amount and timing of the fees to be paid
- the method to be used for the calculation of fees.

Most clients would only deliberately withhold the payment of an invoice as a last resort. This is a dramatic gesture and signals the fact that earlier warning signs have been ignored. This tends to occur at a fairly late stage in the deterioration of the relationship with a client, when emotions may be running high. Yet, at the heart of the problem will be a difference in expectation that has not been addressed either in the original agreement or in subsequent meetings or communications.

One of the many advantages of using the RIBA Standard Agreements is that these fundamental terms of payment are already written in. The client may not have read them very closely at the outset, but this provides no defence later if a dispute arises.

It is a good idea to keep all of the paperwork that relates to fees together in its own separate file. This will ensure that it is straightforward to follow the progress of the project and makes it easier to raise invoices, which will often follow a set format. It will also make it easy to deal with any fee-related questions as they arise.

Late payment

It is good practice to include a note on each of your invoices to clients reminding them of the agreed payment terms. For example:

> Invoices are due upon presentation and payable within 30 days of the invoice date. We reserve the right to charge interest as provided for in our agreement, or interest and compensation at the statutory rate on amounts that are not received on time.

This makes reference to the legal right to charge interest and to claim compensation for the extra administration involved. These provisions are contained in the Late Payment of Commercial Debts (Interest) Act 1998, as amended and supplemented by the Late Payment of Commercial Debts Regulations 2002. The Act allows for a punitive rate of interest of 8 per cent over a reference base rate to be charged, as well as compensation of up to £100 for unpaid debts of over £10,000. Base rates to be used in the calculation are set for six-monthly periods from 1 January to 30 June, and 1 July to 31 December, and are known as 'reference rates'. The correct rate to be used at any particular time can be found by visiting www.payontime.co.uk, which also includes a helpful interest calculator.

Example: Interest on a late payment

Let us assume that the current reference rate is 6 per cent, making the total chargeable rate 14 per cent (6 per cent + the punitive 8 per cent), and the outstanding debt is for £10,000 and it is 30 days overdue.

Then the calculation is as follows:

£10,000 $\times$ 14% = £1,400

£1,400 divided by 365 = £3.84 (the daily rate)

£3.84 $\times$ 30 days = £115.20 (the interest owed to date)

In addition, £100 can be added as compensation for the additional administration involved in the collection of the amount due. The potential cost of the combination of these two elements – £215.20 on a £10,000 invoice – is a strong incentive for the client to ensure that payment is made on time.

The original agreement may have stipulated the terms and conditions under which interest can be charged for late payment. Where an alternative agreement exists, this replaces the provisions of the Act as described above.

Regardless of the approach adopted, there is no reason for the architect to finance the client's business by accepting late payment without some form of compensation.

Aged debtor report

The routine collection process begins with the production of an aged debtor report as shown in Figure 10.1.

FIGURE 10.1: *Aged debtor report – who owes money to the practice and how long it has been outstanding*

	Current month	30–60 days	60–90 days	90–120 days	120+ days	Total
Client A						
Project 1		29,375				
Project 2			5,875			
Project 3	11,750			17,625		
Client B						
Project 4		64,625				
Project 5	23,500			−1,175	1,175	
Client C						
Project 6					8,225	
Project 7		7,050				
Client D						
Project 8				47,000		
Project 9					41,125	
Total	35,250	101,050	5,875	63,450	50,525	256,150
Percentage of total	14	39	2	25	20	

Contrary to the opinion of some of my creative colleagues, this is not about the amounts owed to us by wizened old men with long white beards, it is actually about how long each particular invoice has been outstanding. This is the credit controller's favourite report. It shows who owes money to the practice and, crucially, the length of time for which it has been outstanding. Most practices will set targets in percentage terms; for example, to ensure that 75 per cent of the total amount owed is received within 30 days.

All good accounting software packages will include the aged debtor report as one of their standard reports.

This is where standardised systems of credit control will come into their own. Outstanding invoices should be chased soon after they have passed their expected payment date. At this stage a paper statement or email may well suffice. If a further week or two elapses, this should be followed up with a phone call. It could be that the statement or e-mail has failed to reach the correct person and this is the quickest way to get to the source of the problem.

As with any aspect of client management, it is important to build relationships and establish rapport. Delays in payment are often of a mechanical nature, especially in large organisations. By building a working relationship with the person dealing with the payment in the client's organisation, we can begin to understand their administrative systems and work with them accordingly. Many people have a system of paying suppliers on a monthly payment 'run'. By knowing when this takes place during the month, as it is not always at the end, and by rendering our invoice at the right time we can ensure that we receive our money a month earlier than we otherwise might.

The architect's invoices may need to be approved by a number of different people, both within and outside the client organisation, and this introduces a number of opportunities for the invoice to get 'stuck'. It is at this stage that we can call on the help of our contact in the payments department to chase the invoice through. It is surprising how many invoices can get lost in this process, and it may be easier to fax or e-mail copies rather than wait for the originals to be tracked down. Although the duplication introduces the possibility of the accidental payment of the same invoice twice, this rarely seems to occur in practice.

There is often a spirit of camaraderie between those who work in the accounts departments of different organisations. Many of them perform the dual role of chasing customers for payment while at the same time being chased themselves for payment by their own suppliers. This shared experience means that there is some sympathy for their opposite number who is chasing payment, and an understanding that it is a job that has to be done. Wise credit controllers will work with this mutual understanding to help ensure that the fees of their own practices are paid smoothly and in good time.

The idea is to build up a gradual audit trail. By the time an invoice has become seriously overdue, say three months, there should be a file showing that there have been regular reminders and requests for payment delivered in a number of different ways throughout this time. Should the matter eventually need to be resolved through one of the more formal processes described below, then this file will act as invaluable evidence to show that all reasonable steps have already been taken to encourage the client to pay.

The 'drop-through' and 'multiplier' effects

As a part of the end of the financial year accounting process, we have to take a view about how likely we are to collect the amounts that we have shown as outstanding on our debtor list. Those that we are unsure about, we treat as potential bad debts and reserve against them accordingly. This has the same effect as incurring an actual bad debt. The full amount that is written off is deducted as if it were an expense, and in that sense 'drops through' straight to the bottom line and reduces the profit accordingly. It may seem that an unpaid invoice of £10,000 is relatively insignificant to a practice with a £1 million turnover, as it represents only 1 per cent of the overall income. Yet, if this practice averages a 10 per cent profit before tax (i.e. £100,000), then this bad debt adjustment of £10,000 now causes a 10 per cent reduction in pre-tax profit.

To look at this another way, a £10,000 bad debt is equivalent to the profit that is earned on £100,000 of turnover. This situation is known as 'the multiplier effect'. So, replacing the profit that we have lost by failing to collect this debt will mean that the practice will need to generate another £100,000 of work in order to put itself back into the same financial position. When viewed in this context we can see how important it is to pursue all of the amounts that are due, no matter how small. If we have done the work, surely it is only fair that we receive payment for it. By failing to collect all that is due, we may be reducing our profits by 20 per cent or more.

Resolving fee problems

When it becomes clear that the issue of an unpaid fee is not going to be resolved by discussion or negotiation between the parties, there are a number of other, more formal ways, to solve the problem.

Mediation

Mediation is an alternative to adjudication, arbitration and litigation. It is an informal process that does not impose a resolution to a dispute and only becomes binding with the consent of all of the parties. Mediation allows the parties the freedom to explore ways of settling the dispute with the assistance of an impartial and independent person (the Mediator). It is essentially a process in which the Mediator assists in negotiations between the parties to arrive at a settlement.

The overall intention of Mediation is to reach an agreed solution. If that proves to be impossible then the Mediator will attempt to narrow the issues and, if requested to do so by the parties, will make a recommendation as to how the dispute might be settled. The recommendation is in no way binding unless the parties wish it to be so.

The proceedings are conducted on a privileged and 'without prejudice' basis. Nothing disclosed during the Mediation process can be used as evidence in any subsequent proceedings whether adjudication, arbitration or litigation. Nor can the Mediator be appointed as adjudicator or arbitrator or called as a witness in any subsequent proceedings.

The RIBA Mediation Service is administered by the Dispute Resolution Office at the RIBA (contact telephone: 020 7580 5533; www.architecture.com).

Arbitration

These proceedings are governed by the provisions of the Arbitration Act 1996 and the resulting awards are legally enforceable. If the parties involved wish to have recourse to this method of resolving disputes, they need to ensure that the provision is written into their original agreement. In the Standard Forms of Agreement the articles require the parties to select either arbitration or litigation as the final method of dispute resolution.

Adjudication

The Housing Grants, Construction and Regeneration Act of 1996 (HGCRA) gives a statutory right to the architect to have disputes resolved by adjudication. The only exception to this being where one of the parties is the residential occupier of the relevant property.

Adjudication has the benefit of being relatively quick and inexpensive. Without mutual agreement, the issues to be considered and the timescales for making a decision are prescribed. The decision is binding and the courts will normally enforce an adjudicator's decision promptly if needed. However, either party may raise the issue again in arbitration or litigation, or even in a related adjudication – for example, if the client responds with a counterclaim of negligence.

The RIBA's Dispute Resolution Office provides advice on arbitration and adjudication and offers the appointment of arbitrators and the nomination of adjudicators.

Litigation

Disputes can, of course, also be settled by using the formal legal process and taking the matter to the courts.

Credit control is often perceived as an unpleasant task, yet it is vital to the financial health of the practice. Some organisations who have their own cash-flow problems adopt a policy of only paying when they have been chased. If you do not ask, you simply will not get!

SUMMARY

- Good organisation is the key to effective credit control. The process needs to be performed in a regular and consistent way. It can become a war of attrition, and victory will eventually come to the quietly determined.
- New clients should be credit checked before any work begins, not only to see if they pay but also how rapidly and regularly they pay. If collection is slow and difficult, the cost may seriously erode the profitability of a project.
- Most payment problems stem from a misunderstanding between architect and client about what was supposed to be delivered. The more precise the terms of any agreement can be, the fewer payment disputes will arise.
- There is a statutory right to interest in the event of late payment and most agreements will include some provision for a charge to be made. It is only fair for interest to be charged when we are financing the client's business. Most clients detest the idea of paying interest and will tend to pay the outstanding amount promptly when the subject is broached.
- Non-payment can often be the result of an invoice simply becoming 'stuck' in the client's payment system. The credit controller's job is often like that of a plumber, unblocking the payment channel so that funds can flow.
- Bad debts have a dramatic effect on profits as they 'drop through' to the bottom line. Although the unpaid invoice may only represent 1 per cent of the practice's turnover, its non-payment may reduce the profits by 10 per cent or more.
- There are a number of formal procedures that can be used when all else fails, ranging from mediation to full-scale litigation.

Section 11
Leaving practice

In this Section:

- *What do you want from the practice?*
- *Closing the practice*
- *Trade sale*
- *Passing the practice on to the next generation*
- *Taxation*

It may seem strange, but the best time to consider what you want to happen when you decide to leave practice is at the very beginning, when you are just setting up. We saw in Section 2 that the way that you choose to operate and the choice of business form, i.e. self-employment, limited company or LLP, have far-reaching consequences. One of the most important of these consequences lies in determining the method that can be used when it comes to making an orderly exit.

See also Section 2 Starting in practice, page 9

In truth, few are that far-sighted, and the last thing on most architects' minds when they start out will be how they are going to leave. Indeed, most only give any thought to this subject at all when the actual fact of retirement or moving on is only a few years away.

Yet this, too, is an area where great benefits can be derived from careful advanced planning. Given a number of years, we can mould the practice into the ideal shape for the chosen exit route. We can groom successors from within the business or take the time to identify the need to bring someone in from the outside. Understandably, most practices prefer to promote and plan for succession from within.

However, if it seems that the survival of the practice necessitates the recruitment of someone new at a very senior level, this will require careful consultation and communication. No one would like to see the practice that they have worked hard to build up over many years plunged into chaos as a result of their departure.

Careful planning will also allow the exit to be made at a time of your own choosing, ideally when the business is doing well and market conditions are benign. The exit strategy should certainly be a feature of the five-year planning exercise, so that the practice can be steered gradually in the chosen direction.

What do you want from the practice?

In Section 5 we discussed the need to have a clear vision for the practice and to define what it has to offer that makes it different from all of the others. I have never yet met an architect whose primary motivation was to make a lot of money. Most are simply passionate about the sort of architecture that they would like to do and the impact that their work has on other people. As a part of this ethos, they believe that their architectural vision and its inherent values are worth preserving and protecting and passing on to the next generation. However, most would also like to realise the financial reward that they deserve

> *See also
> Section 5
> Long- and
> short-term
> planning,
> page 35*

for building up the practice. Over the course of the years, value will have been added and it seems only fair that this value is in some way passed back to those who created it. In its simplest form, this is expressed in the overall value of the balance sheet of the practice.

There are, of course, ways to realise this value which do not involve the continuance of the practice.

Closing the practice

You could simply decide to select a date from which to stop practising. The outstanding amounts due on invoices from clients are collected and the suppliers' bills and other liabilities are paid. The fixed physical assets, such as property, furniture and computer equipment, can be sold. When everything has been dealt with, including any tax liabilities, the money remaining in the business can be paid out to the owner or partners.

Trade sale

A trade sale occurs when the business is sold to an outside party. This can be a good way to extract the value from the business, but it does require the practice to be in a form that would be attractive to a potential buyer. The value of the business may attach closely to a few individuals and their loyal client following. A buyer would be very concerned to know how feasible it would be to maintain the level of fees that have been achieved in recent years when those key individuals are gone.

A prospective buyer is likely to employ their own accountants to undertake a 'due diligence' exercise. This is not only intended to check the figures that have been reported in the published financial accounts, but also to take a view on the reliability of the forecasts that have been made regarding future sales and profits.

The following are the sorts of factors that would make a practice an attractive proposition to a potential buyer:

- increasing profitability on a year-on-year basis
- evidence of a high quality of service, ideally with formal accreditation
- a history of innovative design
- loyal clients who have given repeat business
- a high-quality, committed design team
- well-maintained premises and assets
- good financial compliance record, i.e. the timely filing of accounts and tax returns.

Passing the practice on to the next generation

The most common method is to find a way to 'sell' the practice on to the next generation of management. This is where the choice of business form becomes an important issue.

Partnership or LLP

In a partnership or LLP this is often a straightforward process and is usually documented in the terms of the partnership agreement that was signed at the outset. The traditional model is for a new partner to 'buy in' to the practice by subscribing a set amount of money as a capital contribution that remains in the business until they depart. For a well-established practice the major banks offer partnership loan schemes, which are underwritten by the practice to finance this commitment. While they remain a partner, they receive their agreed share of the profits made each year. In this way, the value that they have contributed to the practice is paid out more or less as it arises. There is no need to discuss this further on departure. When they leave, their original capital sum is returned, together with any balance remaining on their current account (the amount of any as yet undrawn profits). An incoming replacement partner then subscribes a set amount of capital and the overall funding level of the practice is maintained.

This model operates on a broad 'swings and roundabouts' basis. No account is taken of the consequences of unanticipated events that may have affected the partner, but which took place outside the period of partnership. For example, the firm may receive a refund from a supplier who discovers that an accidental double payment had been received in an earlier year. Strictly, this should be divided between those who were the partners at that time, but this would be too complicated to administer. Instead, we rely on the working assumption that these sorts of events tend to balance themselves out over a period of time.

Limited company

As noted in Section 2, the limited company format is more formal and structured. The ownership of the company rests with its shareholders. These may well also be the key directors in the practice, but there is an important distinction between these two roles. Anomalies can sometimes arise where a senior director, who is an important member of the management team, has a relatively small

> *See also
> Limited
> company,
> page 11*

shareholding. When it comes to the exit process, it is the proportion of the business that is owned as represented by the shares which matters, not the importance of the individual to the management of the practice.

It is best practice to have a shareholders agreement in place that is similar to the partnership agreement described above, which documents how shares are to change hands. Advice from a solicitor who specialises in this subject is essential, as this can be a complex and difficult area. The process is somewhat similar to the writing of a will. Although the primary intention may be easily stated – for example, on retirement the shares will be sold for an agreed value to the other directors – there is also a need to consider other possible scenarios:

- What happens if a shareholder/director dies unexpectedly?
- What happens if a shareholder/director becomes too unwell to work?
- What happens if a shareholder/director leaves to join a competitor?

Even if none of the above applies and the situation is a straightforward one of selling shares on to the next generation, there is the vexed issue of determining the price at which this transaction should happen. There are many ways to value a business and this matter constitutes a whole subject area in its own right on which many books have been written. There is no single standard method as so much depends on the circumstances of the individual business. Accountants and solicitors earn substantial fees from advising clients without a shareholders agreement in place on the way to arrive at a fair value for a share. This can become particularly difficult as different parties have different opinions on what their shares are worth. The shareholders agreement is designed to deal with all of these factors, including a method of share valuation. In an ongoing business a multiple of recent post-tax profits is often used, but there are many ways that this calculation can be performed. The key is to reach an agreed method, to document it and to insist that new shareholders sign up to its terms.

There are also still a number of government schemes in existence which are designed to allow people to acquire shares (and therefore ownership) in the companies that they work for in a tax-efficient way. It is worth exploring this subject with an experienced, qualified accountant.

The above discussion illustrates the practical differences between the LLP and the limited company. The LLP structure is often simpler and more flexible and, for this purpose, may be better suited to the majority of architectural practices, many of which consist of ten people or fewer.

Taxation

Whichever method is used, it is important to take advice to ensure that its execution is conducted in a tax-efficient way. The realisation of value from the sale of a business will be subject to capital gains tax (CGT). Currently, business asset taper relief (which reduces the amount of tax that is payable the longer that an asset has been owned before being sold or disposed of) cuts the CGT liability to an effective rate of 10 per cent for a 40 per cent taxpayer on the sale of business assets held for two years or more. Substantial holdings in investments could disqualify you from this relief. From this perspective you should avoid investing spare cash in property or shares, or consider setting up a separate legal entity to hold the investments. However, the Pre-Budget Statement in the autumn of 2007 announced changes to CGT, in particular the removal of asset taper relief, with effect from 6 April 2008. At the time of writing, the implications of the 2008 changes are unclear. Once again, it is wise to take advice from a specialist in this area as it is subject to frequent legislative change.

Leaving practice is likely to be an emotional time, especially for an architect who has devoted most of their working life to building up a practice. This challenging period of transition can be made easier if the mechanics of the exit process have been thought out well in advance.

SUMMARY

- The best time to plan an exit strategy is when you set up or join the practice in the first place, although this will be the last thing on your mind at the time.
- Most architects will be concerned that all of the work and effort which they have put into developing their practice is continued. However, they would also like to receive some financial reward for their hard work too.
- The practice can be sold as a whole to another firm or third party. More commonly, a way is found to sell the business on to the next generation within the practice. The choice of business form, i.e. LLP or limited company, will affect the mechanics of this process.
- It is important to take tax advice at an early stage of the process. It should be possible for the proceeds to be taxed under the more favourable capital gains tax rules, which, with the assistance of business asset taper relief, can reduce the effective tax rate to 10 per cent.
- Leaving practice is likely to be an emotional event. It can be made a little easier if the exit mechanics have been worked out well in advance. It would be a great shame if the final act in a long and creative career were to be a dispute over money with your former colleagues.

Section 12
Conclusions – why architects go out of business

In this Section:

- *Failure to use Standard Agreements*
- *Failing to invoice for work on a regular basis*
- *Failure to collect amounts that are due*
- *Not asking for additional fees when the brief is changed*
- *Not asking for additional fees when extra work is added*
- *Failure to monitor project costs*
- *Low hit rate on competitive tenders*
- *Poor estimation and negotiation of fee levels*
- *Failure to manage the design team*
- *Conclusions*

The consistent message running throughout this guide is how vitally important it is to continuously manage the working capital, which is the lifeblood of the practice. Construction projects are long term by nature and some can run for many years. Such projects are so complex and involve so many different people and organisations that it is inevitable that the majority are delayed. As a result, the architect's fees are delayed too.

Some of the most common contributing factors to the failure of architectural practices are detailed below.

Failure to use Standard Agreements

The great advantage of using the Standard RIBA Agreements of Appointment is that they automatically take care of the major areas of risk. They have been developed as a result of the practical experiences and consequent feedback of many architects over a number of years. Clients will sometimes have their own form of contract for architectural services that they will insist on using. The reason that the client wishes to use their own contract is, of course, because they have had it drafted in a way they consider to be favourable to themselves. It would be wise to consider the terms of the contract carefully, taking particular note of where it differs from the RIBA's Standard Agreement. The fees to engage the services of a good contract lawyer to review the client's or the practice's bespoke contract will be money well spent, and could prevent a major problem from developing later. The contract should also be forwarded to your professional indemnity insurer for their review and comments.

Failing to invoice for work on a regular basis

The construction industry is used to the concept of payment becoming due on the completion of a particular stage or phase of a project. This is a reasonable approach, as the speed with which a piece of work is completed lies largely in the hands of the contractor. Most contractors are also large businesses with the financial resources to cope with payment delays. Applying the same principles to the design team is harsh. Their fees are now largely out of their own control and they tend to be much smaller businesses with much more limited financial resources.

Consequently, it makes sense to build into the initial agreement a provision for the regular invoicing of fees, preferably on a monthly basis. As the previous sections have shown, our major costs accrue on a monthly basis, so it makes sense to try to encourage our income to come in at a similar rate. By agreeing to a stage payment fee schedule, we are introducing the risk of a six- or nine-month delay in receiving payment for our work. There is a considerable cost involved in financing this sort of payment lag.

Failure to collect amounts that are due

The mechanics of credit control were detailed in Section 10. However, it is worth repeating the basic message, which is to ensure that the money that you are owed is collected. Failure to collect can take a number of forms. First, we need to check whether all the invoices raised and recorded by the accounts function were actually sent on to the client. It is surprisingly common to find invoices lurking in a pile of 'when I get around to it' paperwork on a project architect's desk, perhaps waiting for a covering letter to be written.

*See also
Section 10
Credit control,
page 71*

Second, we need a system that lets us know when an invoice has passed its due-for-payment date. We need a person who has been assigned the responsibility for tracking and chasing these outstanding bills, and letting the relevant architect know if a problem is encountered that will need their help to resolve.

Finally, we need the tenacity to pursue the debt until it is fully collected. We saw earlier how the 'multiplier effect' applies to bad debts so that even relatively small amounts can have a significant impact on profitability.

*See also The
'drop-through'
and
'multiplier'
effects,
page 76*

It may be tempting to write off the final £3,000 that remains outstanding on a £50,000 invoice, but this will mean that the practice has to generate a further £30,000 of fees to create sufficient profit just to replace the amount uncollected.

Not asking for additional fees when the brief is changed

We have noted that, in general, architects are not motivated primarily by financial reward. Indeed, it seems that architects can be the most generous of professionals, as they often seem to find themselves working for no fee at all. Section 4 detailed a way to track the financial performance of an individual project. We often see that our actual cost line is above our planned cost line, which means that we are spending too much time on the project.

*See also
Section 4
Project
reporting,
page 25*

This may be the result of inefficient working methods or faulty resource allocation. More often, however, it is the result of the team trying to respond to a client's request for something extra or different. We are all correctly advised to be client-led and concerned to keep our client happy by answering their questions. However, we also need remain sufficiently alert to notice when we are being asked for work that falls outside the scope of our contract. This is potentially good news for the practice, if the client is prepared to pay for this extra work to be done. If the client does not wish to pay, we should not be carrying it out for free. This does require an element of judgement and has to be conducted within the overall context of the client management process. It is important to maintain good working relations and show that we can be flexible, but we also cannot afford to give away 'the shop' too often.

Not asking for additional fees when extra work is added

This is a similar situation to the change of scope scenario described above. Yet this can be a more subtle situation that is harder to spot. When the brief changes, everyone on the team needs to be involved and the ultimate building or project will differ from the original plan.

In this scenario the basic design is not changed, but the client requests that some aspect of the design be revisited and alternative options explored. We are interested in pursuing this design option too, so we gladly embark on this piece of work without much thought for the time and cost implications involved. Again, we must learn to notice when work falls outside the agreed scope and agree an additional fee accordingly.

Failure to monitor project costs

We are more likely to be financially successful if we monitor the performance of individual projects and the work stages within those projects. Inter-firm comparisons reveal that there is a correlation between those firms that make the most profits and those that monitor project costs most closely. We all know that some projects will not be as profitable as others. We may have chosen to accept a reduced fee in order to work with a new client or in a new area. However, there is a danger that we will allow ourselves to have a 'good reason' for every project to not make the required level of profit and, hence, end up with an unprofitable practice overall.

Low hit rate on competitive tenders

For most architects the winning of a project is the result of being successful in a competitive tendering process. We have noted in Section 7 that we have to deal with the tendency of clients to commission architects to do more of the type of work they have already been doing in recent years.

See also Section 7 Resource forecasting, page 53

We would all like to design something new or in a different sector. It is possible to fall into the trap of bidding for everything that you feel the practice could do or would like to do. Sadly, the result of this will be disappointment and rejection, and a lot of wasted time and money. Clients will tend to choose an architect with a proven track record or a recognised name. Very few clients are in a position to risk the very large amounts of money at stake in a construction project by appointing an untried architect.

The successful approach is to apply for work where you can offer some recent experience or a unique advantage and firmly believe that it is a project that you should win. Ideally, you should feel that the project 'has your name written on it'. This will help to focus the marketing effort and improve the overall success rate.

Public sector clients in particular are demanding an ever-increasing amount of documentation to be prepared as a part of the bid process. These bids are time consuming and expensive to prepare, and you need to ensure that the limited time available is spent well. It can be easy to fall into the trap of being 'very busy' preparing bids and submissions. But if these are not well-targeted efforts, then the majority of the energy involved is being wasted.

Poor estimation and negotiation of fee levels

We obviously need to ensure that our fees are adequate both to cover the cost of the job and to contribute to the overhead costs of the practice as a whole. This can only be done by taking the time to think through what will be involved in delivering a project and, in particular, the level of resources that will be needed. We need to perform this 'bottom-up' analysis in order to know what our costs will be. From this point we can calculate what our ideal fee would be – in other words what level of contribution we are looking for. Then we can take a view as to what the client is likely to be prepared to pay. We need to be prepared to decide not to pursue a project if the fee is inadequate. There may be slack times when we choose to do a piece of work at cost, just to generate some funds to continue to pay the salaries. This can only ever be a short-term solution and will lead to severe financial difficulties quite quickly if applied on a regular basis.

Failure to manage the design team

Clients are increasingly looking for a 'one-stop shop' in the appointment of a design team. As the architect can be the natural leader of the design team, it follows that we find ourselves in this position more often than we used to in the past. There is often little or no reward for performing this additional co-ordination service. Indeed, it comes with its own considerable risks. Although, in practice, many firms are comfortable with a 'pay when paid' approach, it should be appreciated that this is unlikely to be the contractual position. Standard Agreements allow for the sub-consultant's payment terms to be longer than those of the architect, so that their fees can be collected first, but this does not change the underlying position. Where the architect has contracted with the QS or engineer, it is the architect who is ultimately responsible for the payment of their fees.

It is very important to stay on top of the process and to determine that funds are flowing regularly from the client to ensure that all the members of the design team can be paid at the appropriate time.

Conclusions

We have seen throughout this guide that the practice of architecture involves dealing with the problems that arise from projects that are long-term, complex and involve many different people and groups, each of whom has their own agenda. In that sense, it is a profession that operates in a high-risk arena. Yet the traditional relationship between risk and reward somehow seems not to apply. Architects do not rank highly in the league table of professional pay scales.

I have often asked myself, and my colleagues and students, Why not? This is an interesting question to explore, and one that always provokes comment and debate. I have not met an architect or student yet who does not hold strong views on this subject. My own feeling is that, as a profession, we need to under-stand more fully the level of risk that we are asked to deal with on a daily basis. In general, we manage this very successfully and, with this in mind, we should build our confidence and belief in ourselves as a profession.

I would like to see us thinking more in terms of the added value of the work that is done. We should look for opportunities to work in true partnership with the client, rather than being just another item of expense that the client will seek to minimise. As information systems become increasingly automated and knowledge becomes more widely available, the professional advisor needs to reassess what it is that they can bring to the table. The client is looking for help to ensure that their project is realised on time and on budget. They want their advisors to align themselves with their concerns and agenda. We need to retain our professional independence, but we also need to respond more readily to our client's entrepreneurial, environmental or social aspirations.

We should stand back sometimes and try to appreciate that the work that we do affects people's daily lives in a profound way. I firmly believe that we should value the contribution that we make, both in financial and in social terms, and be bolder in asking to be rewarded accordingly.

SUMMARY

- It is of vital importance to manage the working capital of the practice on a continuous basis. This is an everyday task and needs to become part of the consciousness of being in practice.
- Architectural practices can fail for a variety of reasons. One of the most common mistakes is a failure to use the Standard Agreements, which have evolved and been developed by the RIBA over many years. They seek to help the architect in all of those areas where experience has shown that problems tend to arise within the contractual relationship.
- Most other problems arise from a failure to get paid regularly for the work that has been done. This can result from a failure to ask for additional fees when the brief is changed or extended, or a simple failure to collect monies that are due.
- Architecture tends to be less well paid than many other professions. This is hard to understand when you reflect on the level of risk that is involved in construction projects and the long-term effects that the architect's work has on people's daily lives.
- As a profession we need to understand the true value of the work that we are doing, and align ourselves more with the interests and priorities of our clients. In this way we would be better placed to ask for an appropriate level of financial reward that reflects the true value of our work.

Bibliography and useful websites

Bibliography

RIBA Good Practice Guide Series, RIBA Publishing

Keeping Out of Trouble, Owen Luder, 3rd edition (2006)
Negotiating the Planning Maze, John Collins and Philip Moren (2006)
Employment, Brian Gegg and David Sharp (2006)
Starting a Practice, Simon Foxell (2006)
Fees, Roland Philips (2008)

Other publications

Getting Paid, Nicholas J. Carnell and Stephen Yakeley, RIBA Publishing (2003)

Useful websites

Architectural practice

RIBA	www.architecture.com
	www.ribabookshops.com
Architects Registration Board	www.arb.org.uk
Architects' Journal	www.ajplus.co.uk
Building Magazine	www.building.co.uk
Building Design	www.bdonline.co.uk

Getting paid – credit control

General websites	www.payontime.co.uk
	www.bankofengland.co.uk
	www.paymentscorer.com
County Court Service	www.moneyclaim.gov.uk

Tax

HM Revenue and Customs   www.hmrc.gov.uk
This is the single authority for all UK tax matters, including VAT.

Company structure and naming

Companies House   www.companieshouse.gov.uk
Nominet   www.nic.uk

General business advice

Business Link   www.businesslink.gov.uk

Index